Contents

Foreword   vii
1 A New Hope in Campaign Finance Reform   1
   Vouchers Change Donors   5
   Vouchers Change Candidates   6
   Vouchers Change Government   7
2 Money in Politics   10
   The Effects of Money   14
   Call Time   16
   Unrepresentative Donors   18
3 A Brief History of Campaign Finance   26
   The Progressive Era   26
   The Watergate Era   30
   The Modern Era   37
4 Public Campaign Finance Programs   44
   Matching Funds   44
   Lump Sum Grants   47
   Democracy Vouchers   49
   Which System Is Best?   57
   Constitutionality   60
5 Building a Democracy Vouchers Program   63
   Element 1: Design and Establish the System   64
   Element 2: Require Candidates Opt-In to
   Additional Rules   67
   Element 3: Increase Public Awareness   72
   Element 4: Empower Local Governments   74
   Element 5: Mitigate the Impact of Outside Spending   75

6 Campaigning for Democracy Vouchers   80

   The Status Quo   81

   The Solution   83

7 Toward a Deeper Democracy   86

Frequently Asked Questions   89

Notes   97

Foreword

by Lawrence Lessig

In June 2021, the Political Action Committee No Labels had a call with Senator Joe Manchin about legislative priorities in the balance of the year. On the call, the founders of No Labels emphasized the power their group had in Washington—not because of their ideas, but because of their money. The ultra-wealthy donors supporting the No Labels PAC were able to "hand out $50,000 checks," its co-founder, Andrew Burskey bragged. And those checks, he explained, represented the most valuable money in any political campaign. This was "hard" money, money that the candidates could spend themselves. And then to prove just why that money was so valuable, Burskey offered the incredibly revealing picture of just why the economy of influence in Washington gave the ultra-wealthy so much power in Congress. As he explained, most Members in the House are

> *"spending four hours on the telephone, dialing for dollars. And so what [large contributions from donors such as you] does — aside from sending the very strong message that there are folks who will have your back if you take tough votes that by partisan nature that may not be popular within your party [sic] — it also in real life frees them to*

do more work, because it's spending less time raising those funds."

Burskey is remarking upon an obvious dependence that exists with our current system for campaign finance — the dependence of representatives on fundraising. Because of that dependence, particular kinds of funders — namely large funders — are especially valuable. Large contributors give Members two things at the same time — first, and obviously, money. But second, and even more critically, large funders give Members time. A $50,000 contribution gives Members the chance to breathe, and it naturally obliges that Member to the interest or person who enabled that freedom.

No one doubts that this economy of influence affects our politics — fundamentally. There was a time not long ago when the conventional wisdom was that money didn't matter — that indeed, there was not enough money in American politics. But that view today is plainly rejected not just among academics, but also among the public. In a call leaked by *The New Yorker* writer Jane Mayer, consultants to the conservative action committee coordinated by the Koch family told the listeners that it made no sense for them to defend the current system because everyone — whether Republican or Democratic or not affiliated — believed the current system was corrupt.

The key for reformers, then, is to understand why the system is corrupt. And in my view, the most important insight that more and more recognize is this: It is not corrupt because there is money in politics — politics costs money, understanding costs money, and there will always be money in politics, as there should be.

Instead, our current system is corrupt because of the dependency it creates. Members are dependent not upon the public generally, or even upon their voters in particular. Members are dependent upon a tiny slice of the very rich, without whom they have no chance of being elected. Boss Tweed famously remarked, "I don't care who does the electing, so long as I do the nominating." The funders of campaigns are the nominators within our system; they hold all the power; they don't represent America.

He who pays the piper calls the tune.

The lesson from that aphorism is not that pipers should not be paid. It is that we must make sure that people paying the piper actually represent the people.

The idea at the core of this extraordinary book is one way to assure that the piper gets paid without corrupting the system. Many scholars for many years — including Rick Hasen, Bruce Ackerman, Ian Ayres, and I — have been arguing for various versions of democracy vouchers. And as someone who has given literally hundreds of talks around the world pressing this idea, I was enormously encouraged when Seattle took it up. Because the Seattle experiment, like the argument in this book, focuses reform where reform could do most good — not by silencing speakers, not by tamping down on political speech, but by assuring that a wider public participates in the project of funding campaigns so that the candidates in those campaigns remain focused on the public.

Because that is not their focus today: As much as politicians seek to seem as if they are speaking to their public directly, what anyone anywhere near politics knows is that they are constantly focused as well upon what their funders want. Politicians develop a sixth sense — a constant awareness about how their actions will affect their ability to raise money. They become shapeshifters, as they constantly adjust their views to raise money.

This is the nature of politics. We are not going to change that nature. The most we can do is to assure that when politicians are obsessively focused on how they may best raise money, they remain obsessively focused on us, the people. And not just the extremists among us, the most visible in any system of purely private donations, but among all of us, who would be visible and significant in any system of vouchers that assured that every voter had a ticket to speak.

All the words of all the academics could not begin to match the importance of experiments like Seattle's, and cookbooks like this book. These are what helps the experiment spread. I am enormously hopeful that work like this will make change possible. And I am grateful for the opportunity to signal in this foreword as clearly as I can just why this work is so important.

1

A New Hope in
Campaign Finance Reform

W hat is the cost of a free and fair election? What is needed to maintain the integrity of representative government?

In 1888, it came to light that political operatives in several states had paid voters to cast ballots for Benjamin Harrison and other Republican candidates.[1] At the time, political parties printed their own color-coded ballots with candidates pre-selected, allowing poll watchers to easily confirm that recipients of bribes followed through.

How to stop vote buying? Easy: Going forward, states would print their own ballots and make votes secret. Without pre-selected ballots, there would be no way for operatives to confirm how someone voted. Practically speaking, vote buying was dead.

Printing ballots meant a new expense for the government. One recent estimate suggests that governments pay 10 cents per ballot, for a total cost of at least $15 million in the 2020 election.[2] This was the tradeoff—it was deemed acceptable to spend money on government-issued ballots, in order to ensure fair elections.

Might this idea face some resistance if it were suggested in today's political environment? There are those today who suggest the government should spend as little as possible, even if that money is used to ensure the integrity of democracy. It isn't hard to imagine skeptics questioning why election administrators need to spend $15 million to print ballots, when a previous system was already in place.

Ultimately though, free and fair elections do come at a cost. It isn't just printing ballots: States pay poll workers, they buy counting machines, they set up ballot drop boxes, and many include pre-paid postage on mail ballots. In 2017, one study found that nationwide election administration spending totals at least $2 billion per year.[3] All this spending is worth it—this is what it costs to run a democratic election with integrity.

Today, vote buying is essentially non-existent, but we face another problem that threatens the integrity of our democratic election system: money in politics. To run competitive races, candidates need a lot of money: hundreds of thousands of dollars for a typical state-legislative race, tens of millions for Congress, and billions for a presidential campaign.

No one likes to fundraise,[4] but the misery that fundraising induces in America's politicians is not the main problem: Fundraising is a structural barrier to lower-income candidates and candidates of color.[5] Big dollar fundraising requires rich connections. Many otherwise promising candidates know they don't have the rolodex to run for office, so they never enter the arena and their ideas never get a fair hearing.

What about those who do run, and win their race? They don't get to stop fundraising just because they got elected.

There's always the next campaign, the higher office to be sought, the party committee to support. According to one estimate, members of Congress spend up to half their time, or four hours per day, on the phone with potential donors.[6] They aren't talking to the average person from their state or district—asking for small donations would be too time consuming. They only call people who might max out, giving the highest contribution amount allowed under federal law.[7] That means they spend half their day hearing about the policy priorities of the very rich, and thus spend less time talking to average citizens about what policies they want. Rich donors are disproportionately old, white, and male—not reflective of a young and diverse country.[8] They also tend to be more conservative and more politically extreme than the population at large, helping to drive polarization and distrust.[9]

Even politicians with the best motives can have their worldviews shifted by spending hours each day talking to only one segment of the population.[10] Ordinary people aren't naive to this process: They realize that they aren't the top priority. It's no wonder that polling finds increasing numbers of Americans think the government is run "for a few big interests," not "for the benefit of all."[11]

Advocates have long searched for legal restrictions to solve these problems such as contribution limits, disclosure requirements, and restrictions on spending by independent groups such as PACs. These are smart policies that make a real difference. But by themselves, these policies haven't empowered small donors or given candidates without rich connections a fair shot at winning elections.

A transformative new idea being piloted right now — democracy vouchers — solves both of these problems. The idea is simple: The government gives everyone vouchers that they can "donate" to candidates of their choice. If candidates opt-in to the program by agreeing to certain rules, such as disclosure requirements and public debates, they can accept vouchers and redeem them for public money to fund their campaign. Put another way: In democracy vouchers systems, *everyone* is empowered to become a campaign donor, and the campaign for donors starts to resemble the campaign for votes.

In 2015, Seattle became the first city to create a democracy vouchers system. Each election cycle since, every Seattle resident has received four vouchers worth $25 each to give to candidates for city council, city attorney, or mayor. The system has been a great success, increasing citizen participation, diversifying the donor class, and helping a new generation of leaders run for office without having to seek the approval of the wealthiest donors.

Costs of the program are relatively low—Seattle spends $3 million per year on the program, or 0.062% of the city budget.[12] But some opponents still argue that spending public funds on elections is simply unacceptable. Are they right? Is this a good use of public funds?

Just like in 1888, we face a problem today that threatens the integrity of our elections. Back then, the problem was vote buying—solved at a cost of 10 cents per ballot. Today, the problem is the distorting effects that big money has on our politics. For $25 per voucher, we can empower new donors from every background, allow ordinary people to run for office relying only on their friends and neighbors, and shift the policies made by elected officials to benefit everyone, not just rich donors.

Vouchers Change Donors

Before 2015, Seattle's political donation scene looked much like the rest of the country: The highest giving neighborhoods were 31% whiter and 85% richer than the lowest giving neighborhoods.[13] The top-giving neighborhoods were almost five times as likely to have views of Lake Washington or Puget Sound (in Seattle, the richest areas have views of the water). All told, half of all dollars contributed came from just 0.3% of the city's population.[14]

Since democracy vouchers were enacted, this has changed. In 2017, the first voucher election, the total number of donors more than tripled citywide.[15] These donors were more diverse, more likely to be women, and more geographically dispersed than before vouchers. Four years prior, 48% of donations had been $200 or less. In 2017, 87% were.[16]

The need for big change is not unique to Seattle. Across the United States, many cities and states face the same campaign finance challenges. In Los Angeles, the 10 whitest ZIP codes give campaigns 54 times as much money per capita as the 10 ZIP codes with the highest percentage of people of color.[17] In Austin, 68% of local contributions come from the three wealthiest (out of ten total) city council districts.[18] Nationwide, there's no reason to continue a system that empowers rich, white, old men at the expense of everyone else. We can help deepen democracy and expand participation by letting people donate their vouchers as well as cast their votes.

Vouchers Change Candidates

Congress, state legislators, and other elected offices are over-whelmingly old, white, male, and rich. For example, the United States ranks 87th in terms of representation of women in office,[19] while white people hold 90% of elected offices despite making up only 63% of the overall population.[20]

These disparities make a substantive difference. A 2017 study from Political Parity, a nonpartisan research organization, found that female legislators "are more likely to make bills dealing with women's issues and children and family issues a priority"[21] such as legislation "on gender equality, reproductive health, and issues affecting children and families."[22] Further, a 2018 study from the Carnegie Endowment For International Peace found that when elected, "women of color tend to advance political agendas that take into account the particular concerns of both women and communities of color."[23]

Fundraising is not the only structural barrier preventing the halls of power from looking like America, but it is a key piece of the puzzle. Studies demonstrate that reforming campaign finance laws would be a key way to "transfor[m] power inequities...within political institutions."[24] In a 2019 review of first time candidates from the organization Run for Something, fundraising was cited as one of the top fears of potential candidates when deciding whether to run.[25] New candidates would often report that they "don't know where to start," are "missing a plan," don't like asking for money, or "lack the personal or institutional network for fundraising."

Women in politics "consistently report that fundraising is more difficult for them than for their male counterparts."[26] Studies support this notion, showing that "women have a larger fundraising base than men," but tend to raise more from small donors, meaning they "may have to spend more time securing many individual contributions."[27] Thus, many women have substantial networks, but lack the wealthy fundraising networks of their male counterparts.

With democracy vouchers, quality candidates won't have to worry about finding a wealthy fundraising network, because *every* network will be a fundraising network.

After reviewing different systems across the United States, a 2018 study by the Carnegie Endowment for International Peace concluded that "a shift to public financing at the local level would likely benefit women candidates and candidates of color."[28] Outside the United States, there is further evidence: In Europe, most elections rely primarily on public funding, and European countries consistently rank higher on marks of diversity, such as legislative gender parity.[29] No one should have any illusions that campaign finance reform will solve the problems of racism, sexism, and xenophobia that hold our society back. But democracy vouchers can help level the playing field and make politicians more reflective of the people they represent. Fixing our campaign finance system is one step the United States can take towards becoming a more equitable democracy where everyone can participate.

Vouchers Change Government

The fundamental question of politics is "who should have power?" In a democracy, it's the citizenry at large that rules. At its best, democracy is an effective system because if someone thinks a policy is wrong, the best way for them to change it is simply to convince other people.

Unfortunately, this doesn't always work in practice. Since people differ drastically in their ability to donate to campaigns and thus in their importance to elected officials, majority support among citizens doesn't always translate into actual policy. Big donors often get the policies they want, even in the face of broad opposition among other groups.

Picture someone who is passionate about a particular issue. Say that they've convinced their friends and neighbors of their point of view, but they can't afford to donate big money. Do they have any power in our current system? To some extent, they do. If they can gather ten, twenty, or a hundred friends, they could hold a rally or protest, ask for a meeting with elected officials, or try to get attention from the media. Ultimately though, it might not be enough to create change, even at the local level.

Compare that to a single wealthy donor. Whether or not their ideas have broad public support, studies consistently show their preferences are the most likely to become policy.[30] Even the best-intentioned politicians struggle to keep ordinary people in mind when spending hours at big dollar fundraisers or on the phone with donors, resulting in government policy that advantages the wealthy over everyone else.

With democracy vouchers, this status quo would change. In Seattle everyone has $100 in vouchers, so a group of ten ordinary people have $1,000 between them to donate. A group this size will have monetary sway with state legislators, for whom a typical race costs $50,000-$200,000.[31] Over a two- or four-year term, raising $1,000 a few times a month could fund a strong state legislative campaign. While more people would be needed to attract statewide or federal candidates, the principle is the same: Politicians who make policy to support average people will be rewarded in the form of vouchers, while those who continue to prioritize rich donors will face newfound competition.

For an ordinary citizen organizing or attending an event with political candidates, this will be a profound change. They will no longer feel as politically sidelined and their policy views will be less likely to go ignored—they will have more power to become a priority.

Deepening our democracy—extending more power to more people in more ways, raising up the voice of all in the forces that govern our lives, empowering everyone to co-create our shared world—is a broad project that extends way beyond the bounds of campaigns and elections. Campaign finance reform alone is not enough to heal all the ills of our democracy. But it must be a key pillar in any serious effort to bolster American democracy in the coming decades. And among all the forms that campaign finance reform could take, a democracy vouchers system is proving to be the most promising at mirroring the features we love about free and fair democratic elections: inclusion, equality, voice. Like the ballot, the voucher is a powerful tool, distributed equally to everyone, so that the voices of all—not just the wealthy few—can be heard every campaign season.

2

Money in Politics

I s there too much money in politics? One simple way to put the problem is this: For an ordinary, individual person hoping to fund a campaign, running for office is incredibly expensive. Yet compared to the power political offices hold, the cost of campaigns are shockingly cheap.

In 2020, candidates and PACs spent $6.6 billion on the presidential race, up from $2.3 billion in 2016 and $2.6 billion in 2012.[32] Running for Congress isn't much cheaper. In 2018, the average winner of a Senate race spent $10 million and the average winner of a House race spent $2.1 million.[33] All told, $5.7 billion were spent on Congressional races in 2018,[34] up to $7.3 billion in 2020.[35]

Running for statewide offices isn't much cheaper either. Of the 265 gubernatorial races between 2000 and 2019, the average cost was $27 million. In the four year period from 2016 to 2019, there were 53 races, with an average of $39 million of spending. All told, 15 states[36] have had at least one gubernatorial race costing $50 million or more, and all but four states[37] have had races costing at least $10 million.

Most people don't think they'll ever run for national or statewide office, but regular people should certainly be able to represent their own communities, even if they are not part of a wealthy social network. State legislative races are a great barometer of how accessible elected office is to the average person. From 2000 to 2019, there were approximately 76,000 state legislative races in the United States.[38] On average, spending was $160,000 per race. It's very common for spending on a state legislative seat to fall above six figures.[39]

At the city level, things don't get much better. Of course, big cities with millions of people see a lot of spending—Michael Bloomberg spent $102 million ($174 per vote!) in 2009 to eke out a win as mayor of New York City[40] and Lori Lightfoot spent $6.5 million in 2019 to become Chicago mayor.[41] But even in smaller cities, spending is significant. In Reno, Nevada, a city of about 250,000 people, Hillary Schieve won her 2018 mayoral race by spending $242,000, defeating an opponent who spent $147,000.[42] And in Buffalo, New York, a city of about 250,000, Byron Brown spent $763,000 to become mayor in 2017.[43]

To an ordinary citizen with good ideas who simply wants to represent their community, it's awfully hard to raise enough money for a competitive campaign. Yet compared to a government's budget or the GDP of a city, the costs of running for political office are actually quite cheap. In 2019, US GDP was $19 trillion.[44] With all the power it has, is the presidency really only a $2.3 billion job, as was spent in 2016? As it happens, $2.3 billion is the amount state and local governments spend each year buying salt for icy roads.[45] Consider the local level. The Chicago metro area has a GDP of $700 billion.[46] Think of the influence the mayor of Chicago has over business in that area. Is the mayoralty of Chicago really only "worth" $6.5 million?

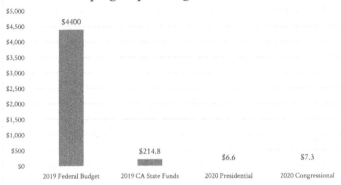

Comparing Government Budgets with Campaign Spending (in billions of $)

Source: Federal Budget data from: Congressional Budget Office; California Budget data from: Office of Governor Gavin Newsom; Campaign Spending data from: Center for Responsive Politics

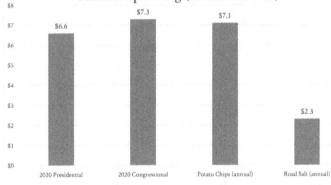

Comparing Campaign Spending with Other Annual Spending (in billions of $)

Source: Campaign Spending data from: Center for Responsive Politics; Potato Chips data from: Hartford Courant; Road Salt data from: NBC News

This seeming contradiction is the central struggle at the heart of campaign finance, borne from the two distinct ways we view public officials. Viewed as economic decision makers, it's confusing how the offices could "cost" so little—The President has a lot more than $6 billion worth of impact. Thus, big businesses and others with a lot at stake from economic decisions are driven to invest heavily in elections, getting a lot of bang for their buck. But viewed as a steward of our government, it's almost offensive to say that a public office is "worth" some dollar number. Public officials are a representation of our shared decision-making as a society. Dollars aren't the right way to measure their value.

People often say that there is too much money in politics. But practically speaking, the problem is not the raw dollar amount. Campaigns are cheap compared to GDP or even to a government's budget, but they're enormously expensive compared to the average person's ability to contribute or fundraise. The problem with money in politics is that people get left out: left out because they don't have money to contribute and get ignored, left out because they lack rich connections that would allow them to run for office themselves, or left out because elected officials don't think about them when making policy, instead prioritizing the needs of the rich donors who funded their campaigns.[47]

The quintessential public good is something that is important yet unaffordable individually, but can be provided to everyone through the collective power of government. As we will see, campaign budgets fall perfectly into this category—too expensive for most individuals to take part in, but easily affordable for a government to make available to its people. This is at the core of the case for democracy vouchers: that campaign budgets should be a public good.

The Effects of Money

Money affects who wins elections.[48] It is not the end all be all—Hillary Clinton, for example, raised more money than Donald Trump in 2016 and lost.[49] We're all familiar with candidates like Alexandria Occassio-Cortez who ran only with grassroots support, and won. But these cases are the exceptions, not the rule.

Donors serve as a filter. As Maggie Koerth of *FiveThirtyEight* writes, "a campaign is like a dinner party, and fundraising is the plates and silverware. You may work hard. You may get a lot of other things right. But if everyone is eating four-star lasagna off the table with their hands, the party will still be a failure and remembered more for what it didn't have than what it did."[50] Money doesn't win political campaigns by itself—but having enough money to compete is a prerequisite for winning.

It's important to note that the biggest effects of money are not partisan. Data shows that the better-funded campaign almost always wins the primary election, but that in the general election both campaigns are often well funded so other factors (i.e. ideology, candidate quality, national political climate) play a larger role.[51] Thus, addressing money in politics would shift which candidates ultimately get elected primarily by affecting primary, rather than general, elections.

For incumbents and career politicians seeking higher office, fundraising is fairly straightforward (if exhausting, at times). But for those running for the first time, fundraising is a constant barrier to success. New candidates report that difficulty fundraising is one of their biggest struggles.[52] On average, only 33% of state legislative seats go uncontested in any given cycle, but 80% are considered "not monetarily competitive," meaning the candidate who raises the most has more than twice as much money as the next highest-raising candidate.[53]

The effects of this structural barrier are unequally distributed. One study shows that at the congressional level, women are more effective than men at raising small money, but less effective at raising big money, meaning fundraising takes longer.[54] According to Shauna L. Shames, a campaign finance expert and Rutgers professor, millennials and women of color are two groups in particular that hate "the idea of having to raise all this money," and don't want to "make [themselves] a telemarketer," thus making it less likely they will choose to run for office.[55]

The centrality of fundraising to US politics causes a uniquely American phenomenon: the enormous number of lawyer-politicians. Lawyers comprise 0.4% of the voting age population, but 40% of the 116th Congress.[56] This is not because lawyers are especially well-liked in the United States (lawyers often rank poorly or last in public opinion polls of different professions).[57] It's also not because lawyers have an innate drive that makes them more interested in public service than any other profession: In other countries, lawyers make up much smaller shares of national legislatures.[58] For example, lawyers (or "barristers") make up only 6.1% of members of the British House of Commons.[59]

Lawyers are so dominant in American politics because of their advantages as fundraisers.[60] According to a 2016 study from Adam Bonica of Stanford University, "lawyers, as a group, are extremely active in donating to campaigns."[61] They also tend to have deep pockets and connections with the business community, which can bring wealthy donors into reach. This creates "an ideal environment to jumpstart a campaign."[62]

The need to raise money to run for office means lawyers and others with rich connections are overrepresented, while the most common American professions[63]—like truck drivers, farm workers, and teachers—are dramatically underrepresented.

Call Time

For those who do get elected, staying competitive for the next election means lots of time on the phone or at events, talking with rich donors. Since the maximum size of individual contributions is capped by federal law and in most states, no single donor (unless they themselves are the candidate) can write a check for a campaign's entire budget.[64] Thus, candidates must talk to many different donors, asking for a few thousand dollars each. According to some reports, up to half the work day of many elected officials is spent on "call time," asking potential donors for money.[65]

Various public officials have admitted that the needs of campaign fundraising took away from their jobs while in office. Rep. Carolyn McCarthy told a story of her time in Congress:

> *"The first week I was down there, we were having a committee meeting on education, and my chief of staff at that time came in and said you have to leave...we went into an empty room and I said 'where do we have to go?' and she goes 'you have to go make phone calls'...This is my first hearing, and you're coming in and asking me to leave? How am I going to learn anything?"*[66]

Here's how Senator Dennis De Concini described his time

fundraising in Congress:

> *"I felt like I was cheating, that I was not putting in a full days' work for what I was really elected to do. I was not elected to come back [to Washington] and raise money for my next election."*[67]

Senator Howard Metzenbaum agreed:

> *"You'd like to be spending your time on legislation—on the floor of the Senate, in committees, with staff, deciding what other projects you want to be involved in. But the end-all and be-all is to have sufficient money to run your campaign. So that which you should be doing doesn't always get the first priority."*[68]

Not only does call time take away from job time—it's widely seen as one of the worst parts of being a politician. Various elected officials have spoken of their time fundraising, saying "I hated raising money,"[69] "It's painful, frankly,"[70] and "it is an embarrassment."[71] Congressman Steve Israel even called congressional fundraising "a form of torture."[72] None of this is unique to national politics—Jim Baca, the Mayor of Albuquerque described his distaste for his daily schedule, saying "I am now forced to spend three hours every day making fundraising phone calls."[73] Many other local officials share similar sentiments.

Perhaps most importantly, time spent fundraising takes away from time with, and attention to, ordinary constituents. This is not a new problem. In 1999, Congressman Tom Udall described the phenomenon this way:

"More and more time is being spent raising money, and this translates into less time being spent doing our duties to support the public and represent our citizens... [fundraising] is putting elected officials in a position of having to choose between spending their time doing their jobs or raising money."[74]

In 1987 Senator Fritz Hollings expressed the same sentiment, saying that politicians "hardly ha[ve] time to stop, look, and listen to the people [they are] going to represent."[75] Congressman Margaret Roukema summarized the problem, saying "Our campaign finance system is out of control. Costs are skyrocketing. Candidates of all kinds are finding themselves devoting more time and energy to fundraising—at the expense of their public service duties"[76] At every level of public office, the US campaign finance system incentivizes candidates to prioritize talking to rich donors over studying legislation, talking to constituents, and doing every other part of their job.

Unrepresentative Donors

Who are these donors that dominate our elected officials' time? If they were representative of the population as a whole, spending hours on the phone each day talking to them might be a good thing—maybe even a way to keep in touch with the community back home. Unfortunately, they are not representative—big donors are disproportionately white, male, old, conservative, and rich.

In 2016, 91% of donors to presidential campaigns were white.[77] Among big donors, the picture is worse: In 2014, not a single one of the top 100 donors to federal campaigns and committees, was nonwhite "by the broadest possible definition."[78] This has serious consequences: According to a 2016 study from Demos, white donors have measurably different policy preferences than donors of color. White donors are "less supportive of immigration reform and action on climate change,"[79] significantly less likely to support affirmative action,[80] and more likely to approve of mass incarceration.[81] Indeed, experts like Heather McGee of Demos have noted the "inherent racial bias" in the campaign finance system.[82]

Men make up about two-thirds of donors in federal elections. Among big donors, the picture is again starker, with women being "the primary donor in 2014 in only 109 of the top 500 donating households."[83] Male donors are "less supportive of reproductive justice,"[84] and more likely to support "allowing employers to decline abortion coverage [and] refus[e] to cover birth control."[85] In fact, Demos described the prevalence of male donors as "a key impediment to more progressive abortion policy in the United States."[86] This issue intersects substantially with race: In 2016, there were more white male donors than there were female donors of any race,[87] though there was a "more diverse donor pool at lower levels of giving."[88]

Donors are substantially older than the general population. Of the "top 500 donors to federal candidates and committees in 2014...only 10 were born in 1975 or later [making them younger than 40], and none after 1985...the average age was 66."[89] Nationally, the median American is just 38 years old.[90] With a growing generation gap in American politics,[91] the continuing power of older donors is a major impediment to passing progressive legislation.[92]

Across the board, donors are more conservative and more politically extreme than the rest of the population. According to a report from Demos, "the donor class has policy preferences that diverge, not just from those of the general population, but often from non-donors with the same partisan identification."[93] Overall, "donors push the American political system to the right" and encourage politicians to become more extreme.

During the Obama administration, the influence of big donors over Congress helped stop or slow down parts of the President's agenda, even when individual policies were broadly popular with the general public.[94] For example, 74% of non-donors supported the 2010 Dodd–Frank Wall Street Reform and Consumer Protection Act, compared to just 48% of donors who gave over $1,000. On the federal budget, 42% of the general public said cuts to defense spending would be their first choice to reduce the deficit, compared to only 25% of donors who gave over $5,000. And on climate change, only 39% of donors who gave more than $1,000 supported the 2009 American Clean Energy and Security Act (the Waxman-Markey carbon tax bill), compared to 63% of non-donors.

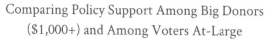

Comparing Policy Support Among Big Donors ($1,000+) and Among Voters At-Large

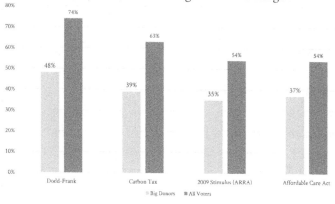

Source: Big Donor and General Public polling data from: Demos

Other so-called Democratic policies were actually popular with Republican base voters, but not with Republican donors (and thus not with Republican politicians). In 2008, 64% of Republican non-donors said they supported an increase in the minimum wage, compared to 38% of Republican donors.[95] Across all policy issues, there was an average gap of twenty points between GOP donor and non-donor support for a given policy.

So why does it matter that donors are nonrepresentative and hold drastically different policy preferences than the population at large? Well, these are the people who politicians talk to for up to half of their work days. As former Congressman Steve Israel put it, "as the bidding price grows higher, your voice goes lower. You're simply priced out of the marketplace of ideas. That is, unless you are one of the ultra wealthy."[96]

Some politicians argue that spending hours each day on the phone or at events with the richest people in the country is harmless. Supporters of the status quo often say that donors merely give to candidates who already agree with them, rather than using their money to influence decisions or "buy" politicians. This argument ignores the effect constant fundraising has on candidates and elected officials, who began to have a warped view of what their constituents think. Senator Chris Murphy put it bluntly:

> "[I don't call] anybody who doesn't have the chance of giving me at least a thousand dollars. So you've got to imagine that the people I'm calling are folks that are making half a million to a million dollars, and they have fundamentally different problems than everybody else."[97]

In his 2006 book *The Audacity of Hope*, Barack Obama wrote that, as a US Senator:

> "Increasingly, I found myself spending time with people of means...[they expected] nothing more than a hearing of their opinions in exchange for their checks. But they reflected, almost uniformly, the perspectives of their class: the top 1 percent or so of the income scale...I know that as a consequence of my fund-raising I became more like the wealthy donors I met...I spent more and more of my time above the fray, outside the world of immediate hunger, disappointment, fear, irrationality, and frequent hardship of the other 99 percent of the population...I suspect this is true for every senator: The longer you are a senator, the narrower the scope of your interactions...The problems of ordinary people, the voices of the Rust Belt town or the dwindling heartland, become a distant echo rather than a

palpable reality, abstractions to be managed rather than battles to be fought."[98]

Worse, fundraising doesn't just change how elected officials think—it changes what they do. Pinning specific donations to specific votes is difficult, but many studies have demonstrated the effects of money on the legislative process. Counter to the notion that donations don't directly affect legislative votes, a 2005 study in *Social Science Quarterly* found that up to "one-third of roll call votes exhibit the impact of campaign contributions."[99]

According to research by Michael Barber of Brigham Young University, the preferences of legislators "reflect the preferences of the average donor" more than that of co-partisans, supporters, or registered voters.[100] In the Senate, "there is a dearth of [policy] congruence between constituents and Senators—unless [the] constituents are those who write checks and attend fundraisers."[101] A 2014 study in the *Cambridge University Press* found that "economic elites and organized groups representing business interests have substantial independent impacts on U.S. government policy, while average citizens and mass-based interest groups have little or no independent influence."[102] All told, the current system "dramatically inflates the influence of only a small, homogeneous part of our population, while limiting the influence of the vast majority of average and lower-income Americans who cannot afford to give large campaign donations."[103]

In a representative democracy, constituents, donor or not, should be the top priority for every elected official. When elected officials don't do what regular people want, the fail-safe is supposed to be that regular people can step up and run themselves. When ordinary constituents both aren't the top priority and also can't raise the money to mount credible challenges, representative democracy ceases to work as intended.

These problems are an open secret. Whether or not they identify money in politics as the cause, the American public is well aware that politicians are most responsive to the rich. Polling from American National Election Studies finds that increasingly, Americans think the government is run "for a few big interests," not "for the benefit of all."[104] The percentage of people saying "quite a few" government officials are crooked is at its highest ever recorded rate and measures of trust in government and political efficacy are near all-time lows.[105]

The American public wants change. According to polling from the *New York Times*, 85% of Americans say the campaign finance system needs "fundamental changes" or must be "completely rebuilt."[106] But amid record levels of political tribalism, racism exploited for political gain, and growing hatred of fellow citizens, money in politics can feel like a small problem.[107] With so much else to do, should this really be the top priority?

Money in politics should not be thought of as 'just another problem' to address. Fixing money in politics is a way of untangling the knot, and making everything else easier. If regular people knew that they could make their voices heard, Americans would be less cynical about politics and more willing to embrace government-driven solutions. And if getting elected didn't mean spending hours calling rich donors every day, we would have better representation of marginalized communities, because people from those communities would be more likely to run for office themselves.

Winning elections isn't enough to make big changes— elected officials need the faith and support of the public. That means reducing the influence of big donors and increasing the influence of small donors, and those who have never given before. It means making sure politicians talk to everyone, no matter how rich or poor. And it means empowering new politicians—allowing regular people to run for office by removing the structural fundraising barriers that currently stop them.

3

A Brief History of Campaign Finance

Since the founding, American reformers have worked to extend more political power to more people in more ways. As with other pillars of this project, such as voting and civil rights, efforts to address money in politics have advanced in fits and starts. Often, significant campaign finance reform legislation has come after major scandals, only to slowly get chipped away over the ensuing years.

The Progressive Era

The first major, modern campaign finance scandal was in 1904, when news broke that President Theodore Roosevelt's campaign had accepted money from several big businesses, and that Roosevelt had allegedly promised an ambassadorship in exchange for a $200,000 donation.[108] A Senate investigation in 1912 would uncover that 62% of Roosevelt's campaign money had come from "twenty-four of Wall Street's biggest financiers."[109] Robert E. Mutch, a campaign finance expert and author of *Buying the Vote*, considers this the first "modern" campaign finance scandal, because "it was about where the money came from, rather than where it was spent."[110] In some ways, the scandal was about decorum in addition to power, since many Americans believed that asking for money was beneath a President.[111]

Two powerful legislators, Senator William Chandler and Representative Perry Belmont, responded by founding the National Publicity Bill Organization (NPBO), the first organization ever created to advocate for campaign finance reform.[112] The NPBO aimed to advance two major reforms: a bill to stop big businesses from donating to campaigns, and a bill mandating disclosure of campaign funds.[113] Since these original proposals, the twin ideas of restrictions on donations and requirements for disclosure have defined much of the campaign finance conversation. Public support for the ideas grew steadily over time, as the NPBO attracted new members, including many politicians and the National Civic Federation, the nation's biggest business league.[114]

Early Legislation

In 1907, the Tillman Act banned "corporations and banks chartered by the federal government" from donating to political candidates.[115] The act also explicitly stated that corporations did not have the political rights of US citizens.[116] Public advocacy was key for the passage of the Tillman Act. Both the *New York Times* and the conservative *New York Tribune* supported the legislation, respectively saying that it was "an excellent and comprehensive measure"[117] and supported "the basic principle of democracy."[118] Scholars believe that majorities of both parties in Congress actually opposed the legislation, but felt compelled "to vote on the side of public opinion."[119]

The Tillman Act did not include an enforcement mechanism. The act called for fines and even prison time if contribution restrictions were violated, but until the creation of the Federal Elections Commission in 1974, there was no federal body responsible for enforcing campaign finance law. While there is some evidence that the Tillman Act may have reduced corporate money in politics, passage was "largely a symbolic victory" for the reform movement.[120]

The NPBO's other major goal was a disclosure law. In 1910, Congress passed the Federal Corrupt Practices Act, mandating disclosure for spending by political parties (though notably not by candidates).[121] The law was strengthened in 1911 and again in 1925 to extend to Congressional candidates—though like the Tillman Act, it lacked enforcement.

In addition to the national legislation, twenty states enacted various laws focusing on corruption, some "prohibiting all corporations [from] making campaign contributions," others focusing only on insurance companies, which were central to the 1904 scandal.[122] Public pressure also led both presidential candidates in 1908 to publicly release lists of their donors, despite the fact that there was no requirement to do so.[123]

Early Proposals for Public Financing

President Roosevelt, who was central to the 1904 scandal, criticized the Tillman Act as unenforceable, calling it a "penalty upon honest men."[124] In his 1907 State of the Union address, Roosevelt said that no law could "hamper an unscrupulous man of unlimited means from buying his own way into office."[125]

Instead, Roosevelt proposed a public financing system that would place contribution limits on participating candidates:

> *"The need for collecting large campaign funds would vanish if Congress provided an appropriation...ample enough to meet the necessity for thorough organization and machinery, which requires a large expenditure of money. Then the stipulation should be made that no party receiving campaign funds from the Treasury should accept more than a fixed amount from any individual subscriber or donor; and the necessary publicity for receipts and expenditures could without difficulty be provided."*[126]

While no public financing legislation was passed at the time, the idea began to take hold. In 1912, Connecticut Governor Simeon Baldwin echoed Roosevelt, calling for public financing to avoid what he saw as an indirect wealth qualification that fundraising placed on those running for office.[127] In 1924, the Democratic Party platform included public financing, with delegates writing that "we favor reasonable means of publicity, at public expense, so that candidates...may present their claims at a minimum of cost."[128] Between 1940 and 1961, four sitting Senators advocated for or supported public financing, including big names such as Senator Henry Cabot Lodge.[129] In 1961, President Kennedy expressed interest in public financing and created The Commission on Campaign Costs to explore different possibilities.[130]

Corporations and Unions

Between 1920 and 1970, most activity in the realm of campaign finance was related to ongoing conflicts between labor unions, which tended to support Democratic candidates, and business interests, which mostly supported Republicans. In the 1940s, Congress passed legislation aimed at barring direct contributions from unions and corporations to candidates for federal office.[131] The Congress of Industrial Organizations, a major union, responded in 1943 by forming CIO-PAC, the first ever Political Action Committee, as a vessel for campaign funds. Going forward, PACs "became the way labor participated in elections."[132]

In 1968, controversy arose when a federal grand jury indicted the Pipefitters Local 562 union, charging that their PAC's contributions were illegal under the 1947 Taft-Hartley Act, legislation aimed at limiting the political power of unions.[133] The government argued that union PAC donations should be illegal because "member donations were compulsory, not voluntary" and because PACs were "merely a subterfuge through which the union itself made proscribed political contributions."[134] In 1972, the Supreme Court ruled that labor unions could continue to use PACs to make donations, foreshadowing future rulings that would open the door to more independent expenditures.[135]

The Watergate Era

The next major advancements in campaign finance reform happened due to fallout from the Watergate scandal and growing distrust of politicians in the 1960s and 1970s.

Presidential Campaign Fund

In 1971, Congress enacted the nation's first national public financing system as part of the 1971 Revenue Act.[136] Since 1973, taxpayers have had the option to contribute $1 (now $3) of their payments to the Presidential Election Campaign Fund, a public financing program for presidential primaries and general elections.[137] In the primary, candidates qualify by raising a small amount of initial money (currently $5,000 from 20 different states, from contributions of less than $250). From then on, the first $250 an individual donates is matched by the fund (up to pre-approved spending limits). In general elections, the fund offers a lump sum payment of $20 million (adjusted for inflation since 1974) if candidates agree not to accept any other money.

Between 1976 and 2004, every major party candidate funded their campaign using the system, including Presidents Carter, Reagan, Clinton, and both Presidents Bush. Over time, campaigns found loopholes to get around the fundraising restriction, such as raising "soft money" that officially went to political parties, but was used to promote the elections of their candidates. Nevertheless, until 1996, "public money remained the primary source of presidential campaign funds."[138]

Today, the Presidential Election Campaign Fund is seen as "broken"[139] and a "disaster,"[140] even by proponents of campaign finance reform. Campaign costs have risen more quickly than inflation, making the lump sum of money inadequate for modern campaigning. In 2008, then-Senator Barack Obama became the first major party nominee to opt out of the system for the general election, arguing that the $84 million he would have received wasn't enough to compete with outside groups supporting Republican Senator John McCain.[141] Obama ended up raising $300 million in the general election, $114 million from donations under $200 alone, none of which would have been allowed had he opted into the public financing system.[142]

While the program is still available today, no major party nominee has opted-in since Senator John McCain in 2008. In the 2020 election, Joe Biden and Donald Trump were each eligible to receive a grant of $103.7 million. Neither campaign accepted, as this would have meant forgoing money from private donors. Considering that Biden raised $364.5 million in the month of August 2020 alone and another $383 million in September, opting to limit his entire campaign to $103.7 million would not have made sense.[143]

Pressure for Reform

Campaign finance reformers in the 1970s were not satisfied merely with a public financing system in place for presidential elections. Even prior to the Watergate scandal, public pressure for reform was rising, in large part because of growing anti-government sentiment. In 1970, Common Cause was founded, the first national campaign finance reform organization since the NPBO in the early part of the century.[144] Common Cause played a key role in campaign finance reform both by building visible public pressure and establishing the "right of private enforcement," which allowed private groups to bring civil suits relating to campaign finance law.

Even before Watergate, it was common knowledge that the Nixon campaign was willing to bend or even break campaign finance laws, "end[ing] the unspoken consensus" and violating norms of Presidential behavior.[145] Before President Nixon's

1972 reelection campaign, "parties and candidates largely complied with the law even without any formal means of enforcing it."[146] The Nixon campaign, however, had no such qualms about doing whatever it took to win reelection, accepting illegal contributions from five large corporations.[147] According to Common Cause, lawsuits over disclosure would play a key role in "unfolding the Watergate scandal" and ultimately ending the Nixon administration.[148]

Federal Election Campaign Act

In 1971, Congress passed the Federal Election Campaign Act (FECA), requiring reporting of expenses and contributions[149] and "limiting spending on media advertisements."[150] The act created the "basic legislative framework for separate segregated funds, commonly known as PACs." Political Action Committees (PACs) had existed in some form since the 1940s, but the FECA increased their role in campaigns.[151] While the 1971 FECA was a step forward, there was again no enforcement mechanism. After the Watergate break-in, the Office of Federal Elections within the General Accounting Office (now called the Government Accountability Office) "produced a report citing several likely violations of the 1971 FECA," lamenting their lack of enforcement powers, a problem in campaign finance law dating back to the 1907 Tillman Act.[152]

In 1974, Congress amended the FECA so substantially that experts consider it "the most comprehensive reform law in history" and "a new beginning for campaign finance law."[153] The law contained four main components: disclosure requirements for federal campaigns, contribution limits on donations to federal candidates and political parties, spending limits for congressional campaigns and independent groups, and the creation of the Federal Elections Commission (FEC), the first federal body with the power to enforce campaign finance law.[154]

While the creation of the FEC was a step in the right direction, campaign finance law often still goes unenforced. For example, the FEC lacked the four votes necessary for a quorum for the majority of the 2020 election cycle, leading to a backlog of hundreds of cases.[155]

Buckley v. Valeo

In 1975, Senators James Buckley and Eugene McCarthy along with the New York Civil Liberties Union filed a lawsuit challenging the 1974 FECA Amendments, in a case known as *Buckley v. Valeo*.[156] Typically when a federal law is challenged, the Solicitor General defends it in court. In 1975, however, Attorney General Edward Levi and Solicitor General Robert Bork refused, taking the "unprecedented step of filing an amicus brief" against the law.[157] Three democracy reform groups "won permission to intervene as defendants."[158]

The case centered on interpretations of the First Amendment. Before *Buckley*, the First Amendment had not often been raised with regards to campaign finance reform. According to Robert Mutch, a campaign finance historian:

> *"The First Amendment doctrine that was dominant before the 1970s had been developed to defend political and religious minorities, who were almost all minor figures at the fringes of society and politics. The point of regulating campaign funds, however, had always been to protect*

> *the majority of citizens against the political advantages*
> *of wealth at the center...Most people would agree that*
> *candidates should compete on the popularity of their*
> *messages...[not] on the size of the audience they can*
> *afford to buy...[however, the First Amendment offered]*
> *a politically respectable argument [to allow for] overt*
> *opposition to [political] equality."*[159]

In the DC Circuit Court of Appeals, the 1974 FECA was upheld 6-2. Not only did the court reject the First Amendment critique of the law, they found that the law actually "enhanced First Amendment values," writing "it would be strange indeed if... the wealthy few could claim a constitutional guarantee to a stronger political voice."[160]

At the Supreme Court, reform supporters argued "that the FECA's primary goal was 'to curb the undue influence of a wealthy few on candidate positions and government actions.'"[161] In a 7-1 ruling, the court overturned the circuit decision, rejecting "undue influence" as a valid justification for campaign finance laws and substituting "quid pro quo corruption" as "the only acceptable reason to regulate campaign funds."[162]

For the 1974 FECA, this meant individual contribution limits, disclosure requirements, and public financing could continue, while spending limits were ruled unconstitutional.[163] The Court "departed sharply from Congress" by defining independent expenditures "as pure speech that had no potential for corruption."[164] Justice Potter Stewart wrote that "money is speech and speech is money [and thus] the concept that government may restrict the speech of some elements of society in order to enhance the relative voices of others is wholly foreign to the First Amendment."[165] Going forward, *Buckley* "greatly narrowed the permissible options for reformers," creating the system today in which contribution limits are acceptable, but spending limits are not.[166]

First National Bank of Boston v. Bellotti

Other cases further limited what state governments in particular could do to regulate independent expenditures. In 1976, the Massachusetts state legislature put a constitutional amendment on the ballot to authorize an income tax. State law banned corporations "from making campaign contributions and expenditures in candidate and ballot-measure elections," and the Attorney General of Massachusetts publicly reminded corporations that they would face prosecution if they tried to intervene in the referendum.[167]

Hoping to "force the issue" and "establish a constitutional right," the First National Bank of Boston sued, arguing that the restrictions violated their First Amendment rights.[168] The Supreme Judicial Court of Massachusetts upheld the law, stating that "it seems to us that a corporation does not have the same First Amendment rights of free speech as a natural person."[169] The US Supreme Court disagreed, arguing that the law abridged First Amendment rights based on "corporate identity," and limited people's "right to hear" all speech.[170] While this case did not directly impact federal law, it is notable as the first time the Supreme Court ruled that corporations had First Amendment rights in campaign finance matters.

The Modern Era

Soft Money

In the 1980s and 1990s, soft money became a concern for campaign finance reformers.[171] Distinct from hard money, or donations given by individuals to candidates, soft money meant donations to political parties, most of which came from corporations and trade associations. Often, parties managed to skirt federal FECA restrictions by raising money that technically went to state parties.[172] While soft money couldn't be used to support individual candidates, parties developed "party-building activities" such as voter registration drives and 'get out the vote' efforts that allowed them to use their money to help their candidates without violating the law.[173]

The saliency of soft money as an issue grew when Ronald Reagan's 1980 campaign accepted public money for the general election (and agreed to avoid all private fundraising), but nonetheless benefited from soft money raised by the Republican party and used indirectly to promote his candidacy.[174] Public concern led Presidents Bush and Clinton to propose reform bills to address soft money, though neither passed. The FEC tried to regulate soft money under existing law, arguing that "parties could not be independent of their own candidates and that expenditures on their behalf were therefore contributions,"[175] but the Supreme Court struck down this regulation in a 1996 case.[176]

Public concern over soft money continued to grow during the 1998 midterms, when a "wave of sham issue ads" aired that avoided using "*Buckley*'s magic words" ("vote for," "elect," "vote against", "defeat", etc.) so they would be "counted as issue advocacy" and could be financed with soft money.[177] Despite public pressure and warnings from experts, Congress did not enact any legislation before the next election cycle. Rather, "the innovations…became standard practice."[178] In 2000, political scientists said that because of soft money, "the FECA's structure had collapsed."[179]

Bipartisan Campaign Reform Act

In 2002, Congress passed the Bipartisan Campaign Reform Act (BCRA), more commonly known as McCain-Feingold.[180] President Bush signed the law in March of 2002, noting his "reservations about the constitutionality."[181] The BCRA attempted to "restore the FECA by banning party soft money and extending federal regulation of campaign advertisements to cover sham issue ads."[182] Additionally, the BCRA prohibited outside groups from running issue ads that mentioned federal candidates by name within 30 days of primary, and 60 days of general elections. Finally, the law raised the individual contribution limit from $1,000 to $2,000 and indexed it to inflation, in an effort to incentivize campaigns to raise hard money rather than searching for new ways to bend the rules.

Soon after the law was signed, Republican Senator Mitch McConnell brought a lawsuit challenging its constitutionality, backed by groups as diverse as the California Democratic Party, the AFL-CIO, and the National Rifle Association.[183] Ultimately, the Supreme Court upheld the major pillars of the law, finding "substantial evidence" that soft money leads to real and apparent corruption and affirming that issue advocacy ads were within the BCRA's reach.[184]

The effects of the BCRA were mixed. The incentive to raise more hard money worked as intended: In the 2004 elections, "parties brought in more hard money than they had raised in hard and soft money combined in 2000."[185] The "flow of outside money slowed somewhat" after the law was enacted, meaning at least a partial success. Despite these achievements, the BCRA was unable to block outside money, which was just "rerouted through tax-exempt groups" like "527s"—organizations created to influence elections which did not face spending or contribution limits.[186]

Outside Spending

Before the 1974 FECA, given the ease of evading disclosure laws, it is unclear how much outside (non-campaign or party) spending took place.[187] Since 1974, corporations and labor unions have "legitimiz[ed] their political activity," leading to more information about the state of the problem. What is absolutely clear is that in recent decades, wealthy individuals and business interests have spent a lot of money to influence elections.[188]

The legality of so-called "independent expenditures," or spending that "expressly advocates the election or defeat of a clearly identified candidate" and is not made in coordination with a candidate or party, has grown and evolved over the years, as various Supreme Court decisions have limited the restrictions governments can enact.

In 2004, a group called Wisconsin Right to Life wanted to run "issue ads," focusing on Senators who had filibustered President Bush's court nominees, some of whom were up for re-election.189 The BCRA banned corporations from "electioneering," or running ads mentioning federal candidates within a short time period before a federal election.[190] Wisconsin Right to Life sued, arguing that these restrictions were unconstitutional. Defending the law in court, the FEC argued that the ads were clearly meant to influence the 2004 elections, not just to advocate on certain issues. In a 5-4 decision, the Supreme Court sided with Wisconsin Right to Life, permitting the ads and writing "the First Amendment requires us to err on the side of protecting political speech rather than suppressing it."[191]

Citizens United and SpeechNow

In 2008, a non-profit organization called Citizens United made a film about Senator Hillary Clinton, who was running for President at the time. The group wanted to "pay cable companies to make the film available for free through video-on-demand,"[192] but was restricted by the FECA, which prohibited "corporations and labor unions from using their general treasury funds to make electioneering communications or for speech that expressly advocates the election or defeat of a federal candidate."[193] Citizens United sued, arguing that this restriction violated their First Amendment rights.

In a 5-4 decision, the Supreme Court declared that the government cannot ban corporations from making independent expenditures or electioneering communications,[194] overruling two previous decisions,[195] Writing for the majority, Justice Kennedy cited "Buckley's ruling that independent expenditures have little corruptive potential" to demonstrate "precedent for giving corporations the right to make those expenditures in candidate elections."[196]

Citizens United was quickly followed by a decision in the DC Circuit Court of Appeals on *SpeechNow v. FEC*.[197] SpeechNow was a nonprofit registered as a 527 group, a tax-exempt organization created to influence elections. They raised money from individual donors, and wanted to spend it on independent expenditures in the 2010 elections, "expressly advocat[ing] the election or defeat" of particular candidates. In a draft advisory opinion, the FEC told SpeechNow that its contributions would be subject to FECA contribution limits and that it needed to register as a political committee.

SpeechNow sued, arguing that "if independent expenditures could not corrupt," and corruption was the only acceptable rationale for a campaign finance law (as stated in *Buckley*), then contribution limits "should not apply to contributions made to finance such expenditures."[198] In its decision, "the D.C. circuit court agreed and struck down the limit," citing *Citizens United*.

The New Environment

These cases had widespread effects on American politics. Perhaps most significant was a 2010 regulation change within the FEC that "cited *Citizens United* and *SpeechNow* to rule that committees formed to make only independent expenditures could solicit unlimited contributions from individuals, corporations, and unions."[199] Commonly known as Super PACs, these committees do not face the fundraising restrictions placed on other types of political committees. 2012 was the first presidential election year after these new rules were put in place. Total outside spending exceeded $1 billion, nearly three times the amount in 2008—and Super PACs made up 60 percent of this total.[200]

Reflecting on the past two decades of campaign finance law, FEC Commissioner Ellen Weintraub said "we've seen tremendous grassroots enthusiasm, but there is no way for the small donors to compete with the influence of the big donors. At the end of the day, somebody gets elected, and then what happens? None of those $25 donors are going to have any real impact on what happens after the election. They don't get a call from elected officials. The big donors, they get that kind of access."[201]

Citizens United has also contributed to the polarized political environment we find ourselves in today. According to Commissioner Weintraub, if candidates needed to fundraise from lots of small donors, they would have to find a message that appealed to a broad swath of the population. But when a single big donor can fund Super PAC ads to bolster a campaign, Weintraub argues that "it makes it easier for extreme candidates to run, because all they need is one big donor to be their sugar daddy."[202] Reflecting on big money and polarization, Weintraub said that "it's bad for politics and for governance because it encourages politicians to run for office who don't reflect any kind of broad consensus about what policies government should adopt."[203]

Disclosure of political spending has decreased since *Citizens United*. Previously, the BCRA required disclosure of the sources of all money going towards electioneering communications. After *Citizens United* and *SpeechNow*, the FEC ruled that groups only needed to disclose "contributions that had been made to finance particular ads," allowing many groups to avoid disclosing their donors.[204] The 2012 election was the first cycle in which the majority of spending was "dark money." Off-year elections saw major changes as well: Dark money ballooned from about $5 million in the 2006 midterms[205] to over $174 million in 2014.[206] Even more troubling, there is evidence that dark money often serves as a vehicle for foreign spending in American elections.[207]

The trend in recent years has been towards more dark money, less disclosure, more independent expenditures, higher campaign costs, and increasing influence of the rich and powerful over our political system. While reform advocates have had some victories, Supreme Court decisions have shrunk the list of options to the point that even basic policies like disclosure are controversial.

The one bright spot for reformers in recent years has been the growth in public financing programs. Public financing accomplishes many of the reformers' goals: It reduces the influence of the rich, allows new candidates to run for office, involves more people in the political process, and has been repeatedly ruled as constitutional. The next chapter lays out several public financing options, and compares the effects they've had across a number of cities and states.

4

Public Campaign Finance Programs

W hile campaign finance reform has largely stalled at the national level, cities and states across the country have forged ahead. Since the 1980s, dozens of cities and states have enacted public financing. These programs fall into three categories: matching funds, lump sum grants, and democracy vouchers.

Matching Funds

Under a matching funds system, donations below a threshold amount per individual donor are matched by the government at a specified rate. Like all public financing programs, candidates are not required to participate. If they do opt-in, they face restrictions regular candidates do not, such as spending limits, mandatory public debates, and increased disclosure requirements. Today, matching programs exist in cities including New York, Los Angeles, San Francisco, and Denver, and for certain statewide positions in Florida, Hawaii, Maryland, Michigan, New Jersey, Rhode Island, and West Virginia

One of the longest running programs is New York City's. In 1988, New York City passed the Campaign Finance Act, creating the New York City Campaign Finance Board (NYCCFB) and instituting a matching funds system for city candidates.[208] Starting in the 1989 municipal elections, candidates for city office could opt-into the system, receiving a 1-to-1 match for individual contributions less than $1,000. $4.5 million was distributed to 36 qualifying candidates that year.

In the decades since, the program has been expanded to add new requirements to participating candidates and increase the incentives to join the program.[209] Starting in 1996, candidates had to participate in a series of public debates in order to receive matching funds. In 2006, the city stopped matching contributions "from lobbyists, their spouses, and domestic partners." The matching rate has been updated several times, to 4-to-1 for the first $250 in 1998, and to 6-to-1 for the first $175 in 2007.

To qualify for the program, candidates must "collect a minimum number of contributions (of $10 or more) from the area they seek to represent" and reach a minimum dollar amount in total money from small donors.[210] Candidates must get on the ballot, have an opponent on the ballot, and submit a personal financial disclosure form to the NYCCFB. Finally, candidates must certify agreement with program rules, including spending limits, to "ensure money will not decide an election between participating candidates," a cap on the total amount of public funds a candidate can receive, and regular audits.

The program has been widely heralded as a success. According to a report from the NYCCFB, "overwhelming numbers" of candidates have chosen to join the program in recent elections.[211]   In 2017, 84% of primary and 64% of general election candidates used the program, including Mayor Bill DeBlasio.[212]   Though some incumbents opted-out in 2017 because of the restrictions the program imposes, 66% of incumbents still chose to use the program.[213]

Matching funds have increased the representativeness of political donors, expanded political engagement, and taken down barriers to entry for new candidates.   In 2017, over 50% of money raised for city council candidates came from the matching funds program (though there is still variance between different areas of New York City, with richer areas giving more).[214] An independent study of the 2013 elections from City University of New York found that "voters who contributed to a political campaign were three times more likely to vote."[215] Finally, the NYCCFB reports that "with public matching funds, ordinary citizens can run campaigns," even "against well-known, well-funded opponents."[216] Candidates no longer need "access to wealthy contributors, party bosses, lobbyists, or special interest groups." Inspiring candidates can build a viable campaign by relying on the support of their neighbors and constituents."

Examples of city- and state-level matching fund programs

City/State	Positions	Match Rate	Requirements
New York City	Mayor, Comptroller, Borough President, Public Advocate, City Council	6:1 up to $175	Spending limits, attend public debates
Los Angeles	Mayor, City Attorney, Controller, City Council	6:1 up to $114	Spending limits, attend public debates
Denver	Mayor, City Council, Judge, Clerk and Recorder, Auditor	9:1 up to $50	Decreased contribution limit
Florida	Governor, Lt. Governor, Cabinet Offices	2:1 up to $250	Spending Limit
Hawaii	Governor, Mayor, Prosecutor, County Council, State Legislature	1:1 up to $100	Spending limit

Lump Sum Grants

The second public financing program type is lump sum grants, also known as "full public financing". Under these systems, candidates qualify by raising small donations and then receive a grant intended to fund the rest of their campaign. Many programs disallow fundraising after the grant, although some provide an option to qualify for additional grants if faced with a privately funded opponent. Lump sum programs exist today for some elected offices in Arizona, Connecticut, Maine, Massachusetts, New Mexico, and Vermont.

Maine is home to the nation's longest-running lump sum grant program. In 1996, Maine voters passed the Clean Elections Act via citizen initiative, establishing a "full public financing" program for candidates for gubernatorial and state legislative office.[217] To participate, candidates must collect a minimum number of $5 contributions to demonstrate enough public support to merit inclusion. Qualifying candidates then receive a lump sum grant, the size of which varies by the office sought. Upon receiving the grant, candidates can no longer accept private contributions.

Maine's program is popular among voters, candidates, and elected officials. In every election since 2000, over half of general election candidates have used the system.[218] 63% of current legislators used the program in their last election. According to Democratic State Representative Thomas Longstaff, "the Clean Election system has encouraged ordinary people to step up and participate in elections at every level. Every Mainer with $5 to invest can support the candidate of their choice, and with enough of that sort of support, candidates can run campaigns that are free of special-interest money—campaigns that are focused right where they should be, on the voters."[219] Republican State Senator Ed Youngblood echoed this sentiment, saying "a campaign finance system that puts people first has many benefits...It will enhance the role of small donors, elevate the voices of ordinary Maine people, and provide a bulwark against the ever-increasing involvement of outside interests in our state elections."[220]

Examples of state-level lump sum grant programs

State	Position and Amount	Requirements
Arizona	Governor: $895,602 for primary, $1,343,403 for general election State Legislature: $18,121 for primary, $27,182 for general election	No PAC/party contributions
Maine	Governor: up to $1,000,000 for primary, up to $2,000,000 for general election State Senate: up to $10,000 for primary, up to $60,000 for general election State House: up to $2,500 for primary, up to $15,000 for general election	No private fundraising
Massachusetts	Governor: $750,000 for primary, $750,000 more for general election	Spending limit, no private fundraising

Democracy Vouchers

The third program type is democracy vouchers. Under this system, voters and residents receive physical or digital "vouchers" that they can give to candidates, who redeem them for public money. Like other public financing programs, participating candidates face restrictions like decreased contribution limits, mandatory public debates, and spending limits.

In 2015, 63% of Seattle voters approved Initiative 122, or "Honest Elections Seattle." Among other reforms, I-122 created a democracy vouchers program to be managed by the existing Seattle Ethics and Elections Commission (SEEC). The program is funded by a property-tax levy of $3 million per year.[221]

Seattle was a natural first test case for democracy vouchers, because of the existing SEEC and the high levels of trust residents have in city government.[222] Seattle also had systems already in place to verify signatures on vouchers, as since 2005, all elections in Washington state have been conducted by mail.[223]

The program was first administered for the 2017 election. Two at-large city council races and the city attorney's race were eligible for vouchers, while the mayoral race was ineligible (vouchers can now be used for the 2021 mayoral race). In January 2017, the SEEC mailed vouchers to 540,000 registered voters (other residents, including noncitizens, could apply for vouchers, but did not receive them automatically). Overall, 80,000 vouchers were used. Across three eligible races, 17 candidates pledged to participate, including five of six general election candidates. Everyone who won an election that year participated in the program.

In 2019, the program was again administered for the seven city council races that were on the ballot. In February 2019, the SEEC mailed vouchers to 450,293 residents. Thirty five candidates qualified for the program, including six of seven general election winners. In total, 147,128 vouchers were returned, nearly doubling the 2017 rate. Across seven races in 2019, six winning candidates used democracy vouchers.

The program's two official goals were to "increase the number of contributors" and "increase the number of candidates." Both goals have been achieved. The implementation of vouchers doubled the average number of contributors, and the program has succeeded at attracting new candidates.[224] Additionally, voucher donors more closely match the demographics of registered voters in the city.[225] The program has also increased political engagement: Even after accounting for prior levels of engagement, voucher users are more likely to vote than other registered voters. Low-propensity voters in particular became four-times as likely to vote after using their vouchers.[226]

Democracy vouchers have also expanded who can successfully run for office. According to Alan Durning, director of the Seattle-based Sightline Institute, "the voucher system has increased engagement, and it has made it possible for more candidates to run. We've seen candidates who are younger or who do not come from money, who do not have rolodexes full of prospective major donors. We know that a wider variety of candidates have run than would have run before."[227] The candidates themselves agree. One first-time candidate said his campaign "wouldn't be able to persist without the democracy vouchers program."[228]

Independent surveys from BERK Consulting show a "high level of public awareness," with only 37% of residents reporting that they had not heard of the program in March of 2018.[229] Awareness is especially high among people of color, with only 25% of those surveyed having not heard of the program. Of those "very familiar" with the program, 79% agreed that it accomplished its goals in the 2017 elections. Among candidates, support is high, as is optimism that more and more residents will participate as donors in each election, as awareness increases.

What if Some Candidates Opt-Out?

Some opponents view the optional nature of public financing programs as a weakness. In 2005, Mark Alexander of Seton Hall University wrote that "the inability to force compliance is the gaping hole in the efficacy of public financing."[230] But the reality belies this view: Public financing is enormously impactful for candidates that opt-in even if their opponents don't participate. Public financing empowers candidates without traditional fundraising bases to get on the playing field, and it lets them make the unpopularity of private fundraising a campaign issue.

Often, the argument against public financing is that as long as there are candidates who opt out and raise mass sums of private money, public financing can't close the gap. This isn't exactly wrong—public financing *can't* always close the gap. What public financing *can* do is give candidates a chance to get their message out, even if they're dramatically outspent. Money alone doesn't win elections. Other factors, such as good ideas, a willingness to work hard, and charisma factor into successful campaigns. Candidates need *enough* money to get their message out. Then, even if they're outspent, they have a chance. Candidates with *less* money have a shot to win, while candidates with *no* money almost always lose.

Publicly-financed candidates have one big advantage if their opponent doesn't opt-in: Private fundraising is unpopular. Polling from groups like Ipsos and Iowa Starting Line shows bipartisan support for campaign finance reform and fear of the "culture of corruption" big money is seen to create.[231] Many popular candidates in recent years have gained the public's trust by refusing corporate money, relying instead on small donors.[232] With democracy vouchers as an alternative, pledging to limit or avoid private fundraising could become popular and effective. When facing a privately-financed opponent, the line of attack is easy to write: "I fund my campaign entirely with democracy vouchers and small dollar donations. Unfortunately, my opponent chose a different path: They fund their campaign with money from a few rich donors, since they don't have a broad base of public support." *Burn.*

Is Fraud a Concern?

One concern among those newly introduced to vouchers is fraud. Fortunately, voucher fraud is no more likely than voter fraud, posing only a negligible risk. In Seattle, it is a gross misdemeanor to "buy, sell, trade, forge, steal, or otherwise misuse vouchers."[233] Campaigns found to have benefited from voucher fraud must return public money and may no longer be eligible for the program. Additionally, voucher assignments are transparent: Seattle provides an online portal where anyone can check who has assigned their vouchers, to which candidates, and when.[234] These steps have made voucher fraud nonexistent in Seattle.

It's worth noting a case in 2017, in which Shelley Secrest, a candidate for Seattle City Council, was accused by her former campaign manager of donating $560 of her own money to her campaign but recording it as if 56 different people contributed. According to the accusation, Secrest was trying to qualify for the democracy vouchers program, which requires candidates to reach a threshold number of small donations. Seattle eventually reached a deal with Secrest and dropped charges.[235] To be absolutely clear, Secrest did not qualify for democracy vouchers and never received any public funds from the city of Seattle.[236] The alleged fraud happened while she was trying to qualify for the program. There has never been a case of fraud within the program.

Is It Too Expensive?

Another concern about democracy vouchers is the cost. Fortunately, there are several built-in limitations on the cost of the system. First, not every eligible resident will use their vouchers. In 2017 and 2019, participation rates in Seattle were 3.8%[237] and 8.5%[238] respectively, an increase in donor participation from before vouchers, but not a significant burden on the city's ability to pay. Conservatively assuming 20% participation and an additional 25% overhead, program costs would be less than a quarter of a percent of total state operating funds in all 50 states.[239] Second, voucher candidates face a cap on their total spending, as detailed in the next chapter, meaning the number of vouchers any candidate can redeem is limited. As a final stop-gap, states can impose reasonable limits on total public spending each cycle. For example, before each election cycle, the Seattle Ethics & Elections Commission announces the maximum they will spend on redeemed vouchers; candidates and the public are notified if that limit is reached (though this has never happened). In Seattle, these measures have kept the program cost to about $3 million per year, or 0.062% of the city's budget.[240]

Will Independent Expenditures Dwarf Public Money?

In the post-*Citizens United* era, there is understandable concern that any attempt at establishing a public financing system is futile, given the ability of PACs and other outside groups to flood elections with independent expenditures. Fortunately, democracy vouchers have already demonstrated the ability to stand up against big outside spending.

In May of 2018, the Seattle City Council passed a "head tax" of $275 per employee on large corporations, intended to fund additional services for Seattle's homeless population.[241] Only one month later, facing substantial pressure from Amazon and other big companies, the City Council repealed the legislation.

The next year, in large part because of concern over the head tax, Amazon spent $1.45 million on Seattle city-council elections, which the *Seattle Times* called an "unprecedented" amount of money.[242] The money went to a PAC "associated with the Seattle Metropolitan Chamber of Commerce" which spent it mostly on paid canvassing staff and direct-mail advertisements.[243] Councilmember Kshama Sawant, who had supported the head tax, accused Amazon CEO Jeff Bezos of trying to "buy this election,"[244] saying "the question is: Is Seattle going to become a playground for only the very wealthy, or is it going to be a city that serves the needs of ordinary people?"[245]

Seven of Seattle's nine City Council seats were on the ballot in 2019, including the seats of Councilmembers Kshama Sawant and Lisa Herbold, the lead proponents of the head tax.[246] Amazon supported opponents of Sawant and Herbold, as well as candidates for several other seats. Several incumbents expressed concern about Amazon's spending. Sawant chose to opt out of democracy vouchers, fearing she risked "being heavily outspent."[247] Herbold used democracy vouchers, as did eleven other general election candidates.

Despite the concern, democracy vouchers worked. Councilmember Lisa Herbold won her race as did five other candidates who used democracy vouchers, all but one of whom were opposed by Amazon. In the end, just one corporate-backed candidate got elected — in a race where progressives joined Amazon to oppose a far-right candidate.[248]

After the election, *The American Prospect* wrote that "Amazon's political expenditures backfired spectacularly. Instead of swaying a majority of voters, the behemoth's outrageous money drop ended up drawing outsized attention to the elections and sparked outrage."[249] Voter turnout swelled to 55%, a large number for an election in an odd year, nine points up four years prior.[250] According to Alan Durning, director of the Sightline Institute, "the independent spending in Seattle seemed to make very little difference. The big bundles of money that went into supporting various candidates, in most cases, they just lost."[251]

Historically, outside spending has had big effects, particularly in local races. In presidential campaigns, "certain candidates have so inspired small donors that they've been able to raise substantial sums of money. But at the state and local level, it's really hard to generate enough enthusiasm to fully fund a competitive political campaign just from small donor contributions."[252]

In Seattle, grassroots candidates were outspent by large corporations, and won anyway. Why was Seattle different?

Even if a candidate is outspent, they can still win if they reach the minimum resource level needed to get their message out. Democracy vouchers don't make everything equal, but because candidates have the chance to express their ideas, voters have the chance to freely make up their minds. In other words, a successful system doesn't need to turn voucher candidates into the New York Yankees, it just needs to get them on the field.[253] According to *The American Prospect*, the 2019 elections "showcased the ability of Seattle's novel public campaign finance system—when combined with traditional small donations—to weather an influx of independent expenditures."[254]

Which System Is Best?

Matching funds and lump sum programs are positive steps that improve campaign finance. Ideally, candidates could use these programs to fund their campaigns and focus their attention on engaging the most people possible in the political process, rather than on raising large donations. But a good campaign finance system shouldn't rely on the goodwill of campaigns—it should create the right rules and incentives to make engaging the broadest possible group of the people the most strategic choice. Matching funds and lump sum programs don't do this—they leave many people out, making it harder than it should be to become a donor or a candidate.

Consider the incentive structure for a candidate in a lump sum program. After collecting enough seed money, campaigns get a check from the government and no longer have to fundraise. Ideally, this frees campaigns to focus all their efforts on voter persuasion and mobilization. Who is a campaign going to focus on in this situation? Two groups: voters who can be persuaded to support a candidate, and voters who need a small push to make sure they vote. Who gets ignored? People who don't normally participate in politics and aren't likely to vote—the very people that a good system should strive to engage.

Democracy vouchers incentivize candidates to talk to anyone and everyone who might support their message, even if they're from a population that is traditionally less likely to vote. In 2017, Jon Grant, a candidate for the Seattle City Council funded his campaign with a significant number of democracy vouchers from Seattle's homeless population.[255] Funding a campaign with support from the homeless was completely unprecedented in American politics—only democracy vouchers made this possible.

Would a candidate under a lump sum program engage the homeless, or any disadvantaged, disempowered group like Jon Grant did? Maybe. There will always be enterprising candidates, looking for new sources of votes. But since voter turnout among the homeless averages just 10%, most campaigns will view this as a waste of time.[256] Lump sum programs don't create any incentives for candidates to engage in this sort of outreach.

Matching funds don't address this either. In New York City, nothing past $175 is matched, so campaigns are incentivized to talk to new people who can give $175, rather than going back to regular donors, or asking for thousands of dollars upfront. But not everyone can donate $175—in fact not everyone can afford to donate anything. Many New Yorkers lack disposable income and can't spare even a small amount of money for a political campaign, no matter the matching rate. Thus, candidates using a matching program are not incentivized to talk to everyone. Instead, they will aim to find people in the upper middle class who wouldn't give thousands of dollars to a campaign, but might spare $175. Changing the game from "huge donors" to "pretty big donors" is progress, but not enough.

Who is likely to have connections to these sorts of people? More people have friends who could donate $175 than $3,000. But consider someone who has spent their career, say, working as a teacher, who wants to run for office. They certainly have relevant experience, and would be a valuable voice in government. But even with matching funds in place, their connections do not form a useful fundraising base, and their campaign might never get off the ground.

Like New York City, Los Angeles has a matching funds program: The first $114 are matched at a 6-to-1 rate. Los Angeles' campaign finance numbers are incredibly bad: only 11.1% of dollars donated in the 2020 municipal elections come from regular people (as opposed to special interests) who live in the city of Los Angeles.[257] The matching funds program helped a little bit, bringing this number up to 16.7% when included in the count. While still fairly pitiful, this increase at least demonstrates that matching funds have a small positive effect on the relative rates of money from ordinary people versus from special interests.

Who are the Angelenos whose donations are getting matched? LA's 10 whitest ZIP codes have half as many people as the 10 ZIP codes with the greatest percentage of people of color. Yet people in the whitest ZIP codes gave over 25 times as much money, a lot of it matched by the city. Not only do matching funds programs not address the racial donation gap, they could actually exacerbate it.

With democracy vouchers, these problems are fixed. There is no longer a psychological barrier to spending money on campaigns, since donating a voucher doesn't cost anything. Campaigns are incentivized to talk to average people rather than those who can give a few thousand or a few hundred bucks.

Democracy vouchers have shrunk the racial donation gap in Seattle: Donors are now more representative of the city as a whole.[258] Vouchers also open up who can run public office: Ordinary people, with ordinary connections can use their social network as a fundraising base.

Matching fund and lump sum programs are positive steps that would improve the way campaigns are run. They just aren't the best we can do. Democracy vouchers are the best system because they empower the most people to engage in campaigns as donors, voters, constituents, and candidates.

Constitutionality

Public financing programs are constitutional. They have been repeatedly challenged and repeatedly upheld by state and federal courts. The constitutionality of public financing was first affirmed in *Buckley v. Valeo*, when the Supreme Court ruled that "rather than abridging, restricting, or censoring speech, [public financing] represents an effort to use public money to facilitate and enlarge public discussion and participation in the electoral process."[259]

Importantly, all public financing programs are optional. If candidates don't qualify or don't want to participate, they are free to run campaigns using only private money. Because candidates must opt-in, public financing programs often place additional requirements on participating candidates that are not placed on other candidates, including lower contribution limits, spending limits, mandatory public debates, and increased disclosure. If placed on all candidates, these restrictions might be unconstitutional. However, courts have repeatedly held that states and municipalities can impose these restrictions on participants because the programs are voluntary.[260]

Escalating Grants

Courts have struck down specific provisions of some public financing laws, while leaving the rest of the system intact. In 2011, the Supreme Court ruled on *McComish v. Bennett*, a case about Arizona's lump sum public financing program. The program awarded political candidates with a lump sum grant after qualifying by collecting enough $5 contributions.[261] At issue was a provision that if a publicly-financed candidate faced a privately-financed opponent who crossed certain spending thresholds, the publicly-financed candidate would receive extra money, on top of the normal lump sum grant.[262]

Backers of the lawsuit argued that the law had a "chilling effect" on free speech by "unfairly influenc[ing] the strategic campaign choices of non-participating candidates about when to spend money to disseminate their political message."[263] In essence, they worried that a privately-financed candidate might choose to limit their spending to avoid giving their opponent access to extra public money.

In a 5-4 decision, the court struck down the provision, writing that "forcing [the] choice—trigger matching funds, change your message, or do not speak—certainly contravenes 'the fundamental rule of protection under the First Amendment, that a speaker has the autonomy to choose the content of his own message.'"[264] While this ruling limited certain provisions, the Supreme Court was clear that public financing itself is constitutional and could continue, writing: "We do not today call into question the wisdom of public financing as a means of funding political candidacy. That is not our business."[265] Today, Arizona still has a lump sum program for gubernatorial and state legislative offices, though without escalating grants.[266]

Democracy Vouchers Are Constitutional

In 2017, a Seattle based group called the Pacific Legal Foundation filed a lawsuit in King County Superior Court, arguing that Seattle's democracy vouchers program was unconstitutional.[267] The group argued that the program violated their First Amendment "right not to speak" by "using [our] money for political campaigns [we] may or may not agree with."[268] After the Superior Court upheld the democracy vouchers program,[269] the Pacific Legal Foundation appealed to the Washington State Supreme Court.

In a unanimous decision, the Washington State Supreme Court also upheld the program.[270] In his decision, Judge Gonzalez wrote that the plaintiffs could not show the program "individually associated them with any message conveyed by the Democracy Voucher Program." Further, he wrote that "the government has a legitimate interest in its public financing of elections."[271] The Supreme Court declined to hear an appeal, thus accepting the program's constitutionality.[272]

5

Building a Democracy Vouchers Program

This chapter lays out five key elements by which states or localities can create a democracy vouchers system, empowering their citizens to participate in the political process by donating, engaging with candidates, and running for office themselves. The elements are as follows:

1. Design and establish the system

2. Require candidates to opt-in to additional rules before receiving public money

3. Increase public awareness of the program to ensure participation

4. Empower local governments to create their own democracy vouchers systems

5. Mitigate the impact of outside spending

Element 1: Design and Establish the System

When designing a democracy vouchers system, states and localities need to answer the following questions:
  a. Which positions should be eligible for vouchers?
  b. How many vouchers should be sent out, and of what value?
  c. Which residents should be eligible to use vouchers?
  d. How do residents receive and use their vouchers?
  e. How do candidates qualify to begin redeeming vouchers?
  f. How is public money dispersed?
  g. How should the program be funded?

Below is a sketch of how a voucher system could be designed, though all variables—such as the value of each voucher, the date vouchers are sent out, and program qualification thresholds—can be changed depending on local needs.

Eligible Positions

States can establish democracy voucher programs for state elections, such as those for state legislators, statewide offices (such as Governor or Attorney General), and even federal offices for the state (such as US House and Senate seats). Cities can establish programs for mayor, city council, city attorney, or other city level offices. While much of this chapter focuses on cities and states, county- or federal-level programs could follow much the same outline.

Number and Amount

In Seattle, every eligible resident is sent four vouchers via mail and e-mail, worth $25 each in public campaign funds. Other proposals have included a single $25 voucher, two vouchers worth $50, etc. In Seattle, most residents give all four vouchers to the same candidate, so few donors would be affected if the program switched to a single $100 voucher, rather than four $25 vouchers.[273] Thus, it may make sense for future programs to use fewer vouchers worth a larger dollar amount to decrease administrative costs. States should also consider tying the value of vouchers to inflation or to an index of campaign spending, to ensure the program remains useful in years to come.

Eligibility

Vouchers can go to anyone who can donate to campaigns—not solely registered voters. Currently, all US citizens, US nationals, and lawful permanent residents can donate.[274] In Seattle, citizens and permanent residents can use vouchers, as long as they are 18 by Election Day and reside in the city. Registered voters receive physical vouchers automatically in the mail, while other Seattle residents can apply to receive vouchers online.[275] In federal elections and in most states, minors can contribute to campaigns as well, so it would be reasonable for future programs to give vouchers to every resident 16 and older.

Using Vouchers

Residents can make use of their vouchers by: (1) Assigning them to a candidate and returning them to the city or state through the mail; (2) Assigning them to a candidate and submitting them to the city or state through an online portal; or (3) Digitally or physically giving them to a candidate directly for that candidate to redeem with the city or state.

In Seattle, enterprising campaigns have found creative ways to interact with city residents and solicit their democracy vouchers. For example, Andrew Grant Houston's 2021 mayoral campaign sends campaign workers to stand on sidewalks and meet passersby, discussing city policy and ultimately asking for their vouchers.[276]

Qualification

To begin soliciting, receiving, and redeeming vouchers, candidates need to qualify for and register with the program. First, candidates demonstrate viability by receiving a certain number of donations of a minimum size (e.g. "at least $5 from at least 0.1% the number of registered voters in the area they are running to represent"). Next, they need to get on the ballot (and be opposed). Finally, they formally opt-in to the program, by signing a contract with the relevant governmental body that binds them to program rules (enumerated in Element 2).

Redeeming Payments

After qualifying for the voucher program, candidates can begin redeeming their vouchers for public money. To reduce administrative costs, money could be given to candidates weekly or every other week, though the process could be quickened with a more robust digital transfers system (such as a public payments platform).[277]

Funding

Possible funding sources for a democracy voucher program include an allocation from the state or locality's general fund or a new levy directed to the program. Seattle voters, for example, passed a 10-year property tax levy of $3 million per year to fund their program, costing the average homeowner $8 per year.[278] A 2016 statewide Washington ballot initiative to implement vouchers would have raised $173.2 million over 6 years by repealing the non-resident sales tax exemption.[279]

Element 2: Require Candidates Opt-In to Additional Rules

An added benefit of a voucher program is the ability to require that participating candidates abide by certain rules, such as contribution limits, spending limits, and participation in public debates. Courts have repeatedly held that states and municipalities can impose these restrictions on voucher program participants because the program is voluntary.[280] In Seattle, these restrictions are monitored and enforced by the Seattle Ethics and Elections Commission (SEEC). Other states and localities should create or designate a government body to monitor compliance and enforce restrictions.

Contribution Limits

Most proponents believe that voucher candidates should be allowed to accept private contributions in addition to what they receive in vouchers.[281] Most also believe that a voucher program should impose significant limits on those donations, so as to ensure the public voucher system is not simply a marginal supplement to a private fundraising race that has the same dynamics the voucher system is trying to disrupt. One possibility, for example, is to have voucher program participants be limited to half their normal contribution limits for the race.

This limitation can also apply to a candidate's own money. A voucher program, for example, could limit voucher candidates to treat themselves as any other contributor—i.e. candidates can give themselves their own vouchers and spend additionally up to the individual contribution limit.

Spending Limits

Voucher programs can cap total campaign spending by a voucher candidate. While it is important to cap spending to ensure reasonable limits on the use of public money, it is also important to make the program generous enough that candidates choose to participate. States and localities should look to past campaigns to set spending limits, and be ready to update after each election. For example, the spending cap could be set at the 80th percentile of what successful campaigns for a given office have spent in recent elections.

Disclosure Requirements

Voucher programs can place disclosure requirements on participating candidates, beyond those required of all candidates. Voucher candidates, for example, should be subject to regular audits, to confirm they are following program rules. Additionally, voucher donations should be public information, made available via a website to ensure maximum transparency.[282]

Public Debates

In the interest of civil discourse, voucher candidates can be required to take part in public debates for both the primary and general election. Non-voucher candidates could be invited but cannot be required to attend. If no opponent chooses to attend, voucher candidates could be required instead to hold a publicly accessible town-hall style event.

PAC Money

Voucher candidates can be prohibited from accepting money from PACs and corporations. With such a requirement, the only legal sources of funding for voucher candidates would be vouchers (redeemed for public money) and contributions from individuals up to the voucher candidate contribution limit.

Trigger Mechanisms

Ideally, every candidate would participate in the voucher program and voluntarily take on the civically beneficial rules that come with participation. However, when one candidate does not participate, the program should be designed so as not to be a liability for their opponents who do participate. Candidates need to see the program as something that could help them win, rather than an unnecessary burden on their campaign.

Trigger mechanisms allow voucher candidates to resume private fundraising beyond normal voucher candidate limits if a non-voucher opponent passes certain spending levels. Trigger mechanisms should also account for independent spending on behalf of one candidate or against another.

For example, if spending by a voucher candidate's opponent exceeds a certain level, then once the voucher candidate raises enough to reach their spending limit, they should be released from all program rules and treated like a non-voucher candidate. In this situation, they could not redeem more vouchers, but they could exceed the spending limit, raise contributions up to the legal non-voucher limit, and take corporate or PAC money up to legal amounts for non-voucher candidates. Conversely, if a voucher candidate's opponent does not exceed the spending limit, the voucher candidate would have to follow the program rules for the entire election cycle. Similarly, if two voucher candidates face one another, they would both have to follow program rules throughout the entire cycle.

Importantly, the trigger mechanisms outlined here are substantially different from the unconstitutional trigger mechanisms at issue in *McComish v. Bennett*. In *McComish*, the trigger mechanisms were ruled unconstitutional because they were tied to escalating lump sum grants, and thus one candidates' spending led to another candidate receiving extra public money. In the voucher case, the trigger mechanism would result merely in additional private fundraising, but would not result in any additional spending of public money, as more democracy vouchers could not be redeemed.

Penalties for Violations

Buying, selling, trading, forging, stealing, or otherwise misusing vouchers should be made a gross misdemeanor. Campaigns found to have deliberately benefited from voucher fraud should be required to return public money and should no longer be eligible for the program.

Campaigns should be subject to audits to ensure compliance with program rules. If a campaign violates the rules, they should be required to pay back the amount of the violation. For example, if a voucher campaign exceeds the spending limit by $10,000, they would have to pay the voucher program administrator $10,000 (regardless of the number of vouchers the campaign had received thus far). If a campaign takes $50 past the contribution limit from 100 people, the campaign would have to pay the program administrator $5,000. Campaigns found to have repeatedly violated program rules should no longer be eligible to receive public money.

Element 3: Increase Public Awareness

One goal of democracy vouchers is to engage people from historically excluded communities in the political process. If proactive steps are not taken to engage people from these communities, the program risks engaging only the "usual suspects"—people who are already engaged in politics and well represented. Maximum participation requires states and municipalities to invest in public awareness and administer the program in multiple languages.

Focus Groups

At least a year prior to first use, the agency administering the program should conduct focus groups with potential voucher users. Leading up to the first use of vouchers in 2017, Seattle conducted focus groups in four different communities, finding that 95% of participants had not heard of the program and 65% "had never contributed to a candidate or campaign."[283] These discussions helped voucher administrators determine baseline public awareness, opinions, and misconceptions about the program. This information was used to inform the messaging strategies Seattle used to increase public awareness.

Communication and Messaging

On first use, many residents and candidates may not be familiar with the program. It is essential that governments invest in messaging for candidates and for residents on what vouchers are and how to use them. Eighteen months before Seattle's first voucher election, the city began producing content on "how to run for office using Democracy Vouchers," and answering questions from potential candidates. Twelve months before the first election, Seattle sent an informational mailer to 340,000 residential addresses with basic information about vouchers.[284]

Even once residents have used the system, messaging remains important. Each election cycle, Seattle has spent approximately $1,000 on social media advertising (Facebook, Twitter, Instagram, and Nextdoor ads), reaching over 100,000 people, and ~$2,500 on printing and placing posters in business districts. Five months before each election, Seattle launches a "mid-year reminder campaign" to encourage residents to use their vouchers and remind them to get replacements if lost. The city also produces short how-to videos on receiving and using vouchers.[285]

Accessibility and Community Involvement

To simplify participation, voucher programs should have a website where users can learn about program rules and eligibility, apply for and submit vouchers, and learn about candidates. In 2017, Seattle's website received nearly two million unique page views. Seattle also implemented a hotline for questions, which has averaged 1,500 calls per election cycle.[286]

Governments should prioritize engaging traditionally underrepresented groups by administering the program in multiple languages and working with community groups that can spread information about the program. In Seattle, the voucher program is administered in 15 languages, meaning key materials and advertising are translated and support is available in each language.[287] In 2019, Seattle worked with ten community-based organizations, conducting or attending 356 outreach events, including candidate forums, cultural events, and leadership group meetings, in order to access "hard-to-reach communities."[288] Seattle also worked with community groups to craft messaging to underrepresented communities, such as adopting edits from several groups to the non-citizen voucher application form.

Element 4: Empower Local Governments

Remove Legal Hurdles

In addition to states, cities and counties can pursue positive change by passing their own democracy vouchers programs. States vary greatly in the extent to which they allow localities to enact policies without explicit permission from the state legislature. To clarify the legal standing of local voucher programs, states should pass legislation explicitly giving counties and municipalities authority to create public campaign financing systems. While this is not technically necessary in every state, it will embolden municipal officials to establish systems by minimizing fears of court battles over their legality.

Public Financing in California

While 49 states could enact all of these proposals today, California faces a more difficult path. In 1988, California voters approved two competing initiatives in the same election. Proposition 68, which would have created a statewide matching funds program, passed with 53% of the vote.[289] Proposition 73, which prohibited statewide public financing programs passed with 58% of the vote.[290]

Due to the conflicting nature of the two successful initiatives, a court battle ensued. Eventually, it was ruled that the proposition with the larger margin of victory would stand, meaning statewide public financing programs would be illegal in California. To overturn this restriction, another initiative or referendum is needed. The California state legislature should refer a measure to the ballot, giving voters the opportunity to overturn this outdated restriction.

Element 5: Mitigate the Impact of Outside Spending

While PACs and other outside groups cannot donate money to voucher candidates, it is currently unconstitutional to ban independent expenditures—spending in which an outside group independently promotes a candidate without donating directly to their campaign. Ultimately, it will take a constitutional amendment overturning the *Citizens United* decision to fully address this problem.

As demonstrated by corporate spending in Seattle's 2019 elections, democracy vouchers work even if independent expenditures continue. But reformers need not settle—there are several steps cities and states can take to mitigate the impact that outside groups have on elections—and, in doing so, bolster the effectiveness of democracy voucher programs.

Limit Coordination

In multiple decisions, the Supreme Court has ruled that spending by outside groups must be done "totally independently"[291] and "without any candidate's approval (or wink or nod)."[292] Despite this, the Federal Elections Commission has "never punished anyone for illegal coordination."[293] States should create new regulations to strengthen the legal distinction between coordination and independent spending. As proposed by the Brennan Center for Justice,[294] new regulations should make clear that Super PACs are coordinating with a campaign if:

1. The candidate or their agents encourage or assist with Super PAC creation or fundraising
2. The Super PAC is created or run by former advisors or consultants to the candidate or entities controlled by the candidate
3. The Super PAC has any communications with the candidate, their family, or their agents about the campaign
4. The Super PAC uses a "common vendor" or the "profes- sional services of any person" that the candidate worked with in the prior two years
5. The Super PAC reproduces material from the campaign
6. The Super PAC was created to promote only one candidate

Such coordinated expenditures should be treated like donations. Under current law, PACs can donate $5,000 a year to a campaign, so PACs should only be able to coordinate up to $5,000 worth of expenditures. If coordination rules are violated, governments should impose substantial fines (for instance, three times the size of the violation) and "liabilities on any director, manager or officer of an outside spending group for any unpaid penalties by the group violating the coordination rules" (language from the Brennan Center for Justice).[295]

Coordination rules should apply to political activity that takes place within 12 months before someone officially starts running for office. A candidate's former staff should be required to wait at least 12 months before working for a group making unlimited expenditures for the candidate's election. After winning an election, officials should be required to wait at least 12 months before hiring anyone who worked with a group running independent expenditures to help their campaign.

Raise Reporting Requirements

Voters have the right to know who is funding electioneering and issue advocacy campaigns. While federal law requires that Super PACs disclose their donors, the same is not required for 501(c)(4) organizations, leading many rich donors to funnel their money through these organizations to hide their identities.[296] States should extend disclosure requirements to show the people behind these groups.

In addition to disclosing their donors, Super PACs and other dark money groups should be required to disclose the people who run them. Disclosure should happen well in advance of Election Day, and should apply to groups engaging in electioneering or issue advocacy, even if their primary purpose is not political.

Some states have already passed updated disclosure laws: In Washington, state law requires the original source of money to be disclosed if total contributions pass an aggregate amount, even if politics is not the group's primary purpose.[297] States like New York and Connecticut have gone further, requiring the people who run independent groups to disclose their identities.[298] To preserve the privacy of donors who merely intend to make charitable, non-political contributions to 501(c)(4) groups, these states let donors establish separate accounts, specifying their money is not to be used for political spending, in order to avoid disclosure requirements.

Restrict Foreign Spending

In its 2010 *Citizens United* decision, the Supreme Court acknowledged that unlimited corporate spending poses the risk of allowing corporations owned in part by foreign nationals to influence the outcome of US elections.[299]   In 2017, St. Petersburg, Florida passed legislation prohibiting corporate spending in elections for corporations owned by a certain threshold share of foreign nationals (in St. Petersburg's case, if a single foreign national owns over 5% of the company or foreign nationals own over 20% in aggregate of the company). Seattle, Washington passed more restrictive legislation in 2020, banning corporate spending if a single foreign national owned a 1% share or, if foreign nationals held a 5% aggregate share.[300] Proponents argue that these bans are constitutional, because of their similarity to existing rules, such as the FEC ban from holding a broadcast license on companies in which 20% of shares or more are owned by foreign nationals.[301] Surprising many activists, neither city has yet faced a lawsuit over the constitutionality of these laws.

Tax Independent Expenditures (The "PAC Tax")

In its 2010 *Citizens United* decision, the Supreme Court wrote that the First Amendment "prohibits Congress from fining or jailing citizens, or associations of citizens, for simply engaging in political speech."   In the Courts' view, the law before them—"an outright ban, backed by criminal sanctions"—was unconstitutional.

Since this decision, advocates have debated various adjustments to campaign finance legislation which might fit with the Courts' criteria for constitutionality. Notably, *Citizens United* leaves open the possibility of placing limits on independent spending above which an excise tax, rather than an outright ban, is imposed. If upheld by the courts, this "PAC tax" tax could be revolutionary for campaign finance, providing both a constitutional way to mitigate the harmful effects of independent spending and a new funding source for a democracy vouchers program.

While a PAC tax itself has never been enacted, there are numerous precedents in which governments place a limit on some sort of spending and impose a tax rather than a ban if that limit is crossed. For example, 501(c)(3) organizations are limited in the amount of lobbying they can perform. If they cross that limit, they face an excise tax on their lobbying spending.[302] Similarly, nonprofits are limited to paying their top executives $1 million per year, facing an excise tax if they exceed that amount.[303] These examples should give reformers hope that PAC taxes are constitutional and worthy of attention.

6

Campaigning for
Democracy Vouchers

To some, democracy vouchers might seem like a "pie in the sky" proposal: a good idea that might even work, but an idea that voters and legislators would never pass, particularly in purple or red states. This could not be further from the truth, as demonstrated by the popularity of democracy vouchers even in Republican areas.

In 2016, South Dakota was one of the most heavily-Republican states in the country, voting for Donald Trump by a 30-point margin. Yet that same year, democracy vouchers were on the ballot, and passed with 52% of the vote.[304] Unfortunately, South Dakota has no restrictions on the legislature's ability to counter citizen-approved initiatives. Three months after the initiative passed, the South Dakota legislature used emergency procedures to repeal the democracy vouchers program, which was never implemented.[305]

Regardless of the antidemocratic actions of some legislators, it's clear that voters in every state are eager to reform campaign finance. Armed with the proper messaging and campaign tactics, advocates can pass democracy vouchers anywhere.

The Status Quo

It sometimes appears that in our age of hyper-polarization, there are no remaining policy proposals with bipartisan appeal. Fortunately, issues like consolidated power and corruption interest grassroots Democrats and Republicans alike. For decades, majorities of Americans, regardless of political ideology, have been eager to reform our campaign finance system.[306] This broad support exists despite the fact that most voters don't understand the full extent of the problem.

Talk About Donor Demographics From a Standpoint of Basic Values

When campaigning for democracy vouchers, it's important to step back from the day-to-day political fray and consider broader ideals of what politics should be.

Most people agree that there should be local control over local politics. Intuitively, it makes sense that local residents should be calling the shots—they live in the area, they get to vote in local elections, and they're the ones most affected by the decisions. Yet despite this ideal, residents don't tend to give the most money to local campaigns. Consistently, outsiders and corporations are the ones who dominate campaign giving.

Take Los Angeles as an example (though most cities and states across the country follow the same pattern). Donations in LA's 2020 City Council and School Board elections totaled

$31.9 million.[307] Of this, $16.2 million (or 51%) came from special interests—businesses, labor unions, PACs, etc. Of the remaining $15.7 million, $4 million came from outside California and $6.3 million came from within California but outside Los Angeles. This leaves just over $5 million, or 17% of total donations, that came from Los Angeles residents.

Focusing on local control over local politics is clarifying. Campaigning for democracy vouchers isn't about helping Democrats or Republicans, it isn't about national political divisions, it isn't even about one policy versus another—democracy vouchers are about empowering local residents to control a larger share of campaign giving.

Emphasize Who Can and Can't Run for Office

In both local and national politics, the need to raise lots of money from big donors restricts who can run for office. Across the board, people with rich connections are dramatically overrepresented.[308] That means lots of lawyers and business people, but fewer teachers, scientists, nurses, or construction workers. The need to raise money is also a part of the reason white men are overrepresented in politics.[309] When forced to go to big donors, new candidates are at the whims of what those donors view as "electable"—and too often that means white men.

It's important for reformers to emphasize that money in politics isn't just about 'buying politicians'—it's also about who can afford to run for office in the first place. One way for advocates to emphasize these points is to ask potential supporters whether they think they or their neighbors could raise enough money to run a serious campaign.

Show What It's Actually Like To Be a Politician

People have all sorts of ideas about what it's like to be a politician. Some imagine politicians as they're presented on the TV show *The West Wing*—a group of dedicated, smart public servants, trying to make the country better. Others picture *House of Cards*, thinking that politicians are conniving and evil, always looking for a way to exploit situations to their benefit.

The reality that few imagine is how much of the job is structured around fundraising. When asked to estimate what fraction of their time lawmakers spend fundraising, nearly 60% of the public guessed it was less than a quarter of their time, when the reality is nearly double that.[310]

Talking about this side of political life again emphasizes that money in politics is not just about 'buying politicians'—it's about all the ways the need to fundraise takes up our politicians' time and energy.

The Solution

There are many reasons to be worried about the future of politics. At times, the problems we face as a country can feel so overwhelming that it becomes tempting to focus exclusively on the bad. Some advocates might believe that focusing on problems is motivating for the public, and thus the best way to stir change. Just as important, though, is emphasizing the solutions to those problems, and how people's lives could improve with those solutions in place.

Don't Sound Pessimistic

Piling on fear and negativity doesn't necessarily make people become more engaged and take action. They might choose to ignore politics altogether instead. Focusing on problems can be motivating for some, but it's important not to leave people thinking a solution is impossible. Campaign finance in particular faces an apathy problem. Many people come to the subject fired up to do something, learn that the Supreme Court makes many reforms impossible, and give up.

Advocates for democracy vouchers should strive not to seem overly pessimistic, lest they lose potential supporters. Talk about the problems, yes, but never without saying what the solution is and how that solution will fix things.

Emphasize That Public Financing Is Always Optional

Some people have a bias towards the status quo, focusing on the negative consequences that any new system could have. When faced with this mindset, it's important to emphasize that democracy vouchers and public financing generally are completely optional. Advocates should explain that if they don't want to use the program, candidates can fundraise the old fashioned way under the old rules. If donors don't want to use their vouchers, they don't have to—they can still donate regular money or sit out donations altogether.

Put Democracy Vouchers Forward Alongside Other Reforms

One final strategy is to promote democracy vouchers as part of a broader package including more basic "good government" reforms. Rather than needing to explain democracy vouchers in every conversation with a potential voter, campaigns can paint a bigger picture about the need to end government corruption.

The public at large is so frustrated with money in politics that nearly any reform that seems to address corruption can gain popular support. Opponents of public campaign financing used this to their advantage in 1980s California, when they put forward a reform that seemed at a glance to be against corruption, but included a provision that banned the state from enacting any public financing programs.

Democracy vouchers were enacted in Seattle after the 2015 passage of Initiative 122. Though vouchers were the biggest piece of this initiative, it also included a decreased contribution limit for all candidates, a law against paid signature gatherers pretending to be volunteers, and a ban on former elected officials lobbying the city of Seattle for at least three years after leaving office.[311] Many people who worked on the 2015 campaign believe they benefited from including other reforms in their initiative, which allowed them to begin conversations with simpler reforms before transitioning to democracy vouchers.

7

Toward a Deeper Democracy

There's a famous quip from Winston Churchill, though whether he was speaking for himself or quoting someone else isn't entirely known. Regardless, in a 1947 speech on the floor of the House of Commons, Churchill said that "democracy is the worst form of government, except for all those other forms that have been tried."[312]

I hate this quote.

Democracy isn't one particular form of government to be compared against all the others. The number of different ways to construct a democracy is uncountably large, with each possibility varying in categories like the speed at which new reforms can be enacted, the rights explicitly enumerated in official documents, and the amount of local and individual power.

There are many, many forms democracy could take, and to say that we've already found the best one would be exceedingly arrogant. When we see problems in our democracy, we don't need to just accept them because the only alternatives we can imagine are worse. *"Ho hum,"* says straw-man Churchill. *"It's just too bad that the rich and powerful dominate American politics, but at least you don't have a dictator!"*

For a more complete vision, we can look to political thinkers like W.E.B. Du Bois. In his 1935 work *Black Reconstruction in America*, Du Bois coined the term "abolition democracy,"[313] referring to his "vision of a full and uncompromising reconstruction of American society."[314] To this end, Du Bois believed in the need to both abolish old institutions that served as forces for oppression and to create new institutions that could be forces for good. Rather than simply coping with the problems we face because American democracy is already better than a dictatorship, Du Bois wanted to abolish harmful structures and replace them with better, more democratic versions.

Put another way, abolition democracy is not just about ending the structures that exacerbate problems in society, it's about creating new structures that make society better. As NYU Professor Fred Moten put it when discussing criminal justice reform, activists should aim not for "the abolition of prisons, but the abolition of a society that could have prisons…not abolition as the elimination of anything, but abolition as the founding of a new society."[315]

No proposal to address money in politics will ever solve all the ills of society. Yet today's campaign finance system certainly qualifies as an institution that serves to perpetuate power disbalances along lines of race, gender, and class, in all the ways laid out in this book.

In recent years, activists have called for many policy changes to address money in politics: such as ending *Citizens United*, mandating increased disclosure, and stopping the flow of foreign money into American elections. These are smart proposals that would serve our communities well.

Yet even at their fullest extent, these policies merely serve to diminish a bad institution, not to create a better one. By themselves, these policies fail the abolition democracy test: They deconstruct institutions that have caused oppression without constructing new, democratic institutions that can be sources of good.

Democracy vouchers are the missing piece: They give every resident the ability to donate, thus giving every candidate the means to fund a competitive campaign without having to go to the same disproportionately rich, white, male donors. Democracy vouchers democratize campaign finance, forming a better institution that gives everyone the power to participate.

In the words of Du Bois, the soul of democracy is "honest and earnest criticism from those whose interests are most nearly touched."[316] Put another way, the best path to a better society is to expand more power to more people in more ways, giving everyone the means to influence the issues that matter to them. Let's take another step toward making that vision a reality.

Frequently Asked Questions

Money in Politics

In 2016, the Clinton campaign had more money than the Trump campaign, but lost. Why should I care about campaign finance?

Having more money never guarantees a victory, but having *no* money essentially guarantees a loss. Having *enough* money is essential to running a competitive campaign. In presidential elections, both candidates usually have enough money to spread their message, so the race comes down to policy ideas, partisanship, individual charisma, and other non-fundraising factors. Because of these factors, the presidential level is the level least in need of campaign finance reform. The most important changes will happen at the local, state, and congressional levels, where candidates don't always have enough money to fund the basics of getting their message out, like hiring a staff or buying campaign mailers.

If money in politics is such a problem, why should we put more money into politics?

Money in politics isn't really the problem, per se—the relevant question is whether it's private money or public money. With the current system, politicians are forced to accomodate big donors to raise money, and ordinary people know they will struggle to run for office because they don't have wealthy connections. Democracy vouchers put more money in politics, but into the hands of the people, so that anyone can run for office and anyone can be a donor.

Public Financing

Why are democracy vouchers better than other public financing programs like matching funds or lump sum grants?

Matching funds and lump sum programs are positive steps—they just aren't the best we can do because they still leave many people out, making it harder than it should be to become a donor or a candidate. Democracy vouchers incentivize candidates to talk to anyone and everyone who might support their message, even if they're from a population that is traditionally less likely to vote. Matching funds and lump sum programs don't accomplish this, just incentivizing candidates to talk to people who can give the maximum matched amount or are the most likely to vote. Democracy vouchers are the best system because they empower the most people to engage in democracy as donors, voters, constituents, and candidates.

Independent Expenditures

Can candidates using democracy vouchers successfully compete with big money or privately-financed candidates?

Yes. This isn't theoretical: We've seen voucher candidates win against big money repeatedly in Seattle.[317] Getting attacked by rich outside groups still hurts, but democracy vouchers provide candidates with adequate funding to get their message out. This means candidates have a real shot to win, even if they don't have the most money of anyone in the race. Long term, we should absolutely do more to level the playing field, likely with a constitutional amendment overturning *Citizens United* and *Buckley*. But with or without that in place, democracy vouchers can have a big effect.

Cost

This seems like a good idea, but isn't it just too expensive?

It's actually surprisingly cheap. When Seattle's program passed, it cost 0.062% of the overall city budget.[318] Even assuming increased donor participation and widespread use by candidates, the program would still cost only a fraction of a percent of a state budget.[319]

Wait...how can Seattle's program cost $8 per homeowner if it gives everyone $100 in vouchers?

First, the program is only run every other year. Second, not everyone uses their vouchers. In 2019, 8.5% of Seattleites used at least one voucher, an increase in donor participation from before, but not a significant burden on the city.[320] Each election cycle, the Seattle Ethics & Elections Commission announces the maximum they will spend on redeemed vouchers. That limit has never been reached before, but if it was that would be another limitation on program costs.

What if the program runs out of money?

When candidates join the program, they face limits on the total number of vouchers they can redeem, so that the use of public money is limited. Programs have the added option of announcing an overall limit on public spending, and alerting candidates and the public if they are almost to that number.[321]

Fraud

Won't candidates or outside groups try to buy vouchers?

There are several reasons why this isn't a concern. First of all, as outlined above, any jurisdiction that enacted democracy vouchers would make buying vouchers a crime, just like buying votes.[322] Second, voucher assignments will be public information. That means whistleblowers and opposing campaigns can identify violations. Finally, buying vouchers just wouldn't be a feasible way to fund a campaign. Imagine going door-to-door, offering people money to redeem their vouchers, knowing that (a) they all have to stay quiet about it, or you could go to jail, (b) anyone can look at the records for suspicious patterns and can go talk to the people who gave you vouchers, and (c) the vouchers are only worth $25, so you have to do this thousands of times in order to fund your campaign. If you're willing to work that hard and talk to that many people, it would be smarter to just run a legitimate campaign, and ask people to give you their vouchers as a donation.

Political Bias

Is this biased towards one party?

Candidates from any party can use the system, as long as they have public support. That means convincing more people becomes the source of political power, as it should be in a democracy.

Don't vouchers effectively make people support candidates they disagree with?

In fact, they do the exact opposite. Residents can give vouchers to whomever they want, so they have the power to support candidates they do agree with—or to run for office themselves if they'd like.

Participation

What if only some of the candidates choose to participate?

That's ok! The candidates that do participate will be able to run without support from rich donors, and as demonstrated in Seattle, their campaigns will be very competitive. Public financing programs like democracy vouchers won't always be able to close the gap entirely with private money, but can provide candidates with enough money to get their message out.

What if only people who are already politically engaged use their vouchers?

A: As part of the program, cities and states should take steps to ensure that as many people as possible know about and can use their vouchers, like in Seattle.[323] Steps like focus groups with underrepresented populations, information mailers and videos to teach people how to use their vouchers, and running the program in multiple languages, all help to maximize inclusion.

If people don't care about politics, why should we bother trying to engage them?

We are all better off if everyone has the knowledge and resources to pay attention, learn about the issues, and participate in democracy. Our society suffers when only some people are able to participate, while others are forced to sit back and watch. Today, many Americans would like to participate, but don't because they know their voice will get drowned out. Democracy vouchers don't guarantee that everyone will participate, but they remove wealth as a structural barrier to becoming a donor or a candidate.

Complexity

This sounds like a complicated proposal. Won't this be too hard for the government to administer?

There's nothing about voucher programs that make them more complex than many things governments already do. Governments will simply need to keep a list of residents and mailing addresses, and send them their vouchers at the appropriate time. Other tasks, like tracking vouchers and facilitating the exchange of vouchers for campaign funds, aren't any more complicated than other aspects of managing elections. Challenges like voucher individualization, security, and redemption aren't much more complicated than the individualization, security, and redemption systems that businesses use when they sell gift cards.

Maybe it can be administered, but is it too complex for residents and candidates to understand?

The concept of a democracy voucher is no more complicated than a gift card, something millions of Americans use every year. Of course, like any new program, public understanding will increase over time. But in Seattle, public polling found that the vast majority of residents had heard of and approved of the program after just one cycle, boding well for the program's future.[324]

Can It Pass?

Maybe progressive cities like Seattle can pass democracy vouchers. But is this a policy that can gain popular approval in purple or red parts of the country?

Yes. This isn't theoretical—the voters of South Dakota passed democracy vouchers in a 2016 ballot initiative (though the state legislature repealed it before it could be implemented).[325] Polling shows that voters of all political stripes care about campaign finance reform and are worried about government corruption.[326] With the right campaign, democracy vouchers can pass anywhere in the country.

What about campaigns that have failed?

With campaigns for any innovative policy, there are always early failures that lay the groundwork for future successes. Democracy vouchers have been on the ballot five times[327] and passed twice, a good start for a brand new policy. Certainly, the close loss in Austin, Texas in May of 2021 was disappointing.[328]

Nevertheless, it remains true that voters overwhelmingly want a new campaign finance system.[329] With the right campaign, democracy vouchers can pass anywhere in the United States.

Notes

A NEW HOPE IN CAMPAIGN FINANCE REFORM

1   S.J. Ackerman, The Vote That Failed, *Smithsonian Magazine*, Nov. 1998, https://perma.cc/F3PA-HR88

2   Paper Ballot Costs and Printing, *VotersUnite*, Apr. 28, 2005, https://perma.cc/NK7C-4L6L

3   Zach Mohr et al., How Much Are We Spending on Election Administration?, *MIT Election Data and Science Lab*, https://perma.cc/CGT8-7SMG

4   Mark C. Alexander, Let Them Do Their Jobs, *Loyola University Chicago Law Journal*, Oct. 4, 2005, https://perma.cc/VR66-J3C5

5   Run for Something Community Impact Findings, *Avalanche*, Jan. 14, 2019, https://perma.cc/4KJN-K35A

6   Ryan Grim and Sabrina Siddiqui, Call Time For Congress Shows How Fundraising Dominates Bleak Work Life, *HuffPost*, Jan. 8, 2013, https://perma.cc/GFB4-FJX6

7   Contribution Limits, *Federal Elections Commission*, https://perma.cc/XJZ9-R3XX

8   Sean McElwee et al., Whose Voice, Whose Choice?, *Demos*, 2016, https://perma.cc/JZ9Y-ARY4

9   Ibid.

10   Barack Obama, *The Audacity of Hope*, 2006

11   *American National Election Studies*, https://perma.cc/3ZAZ-P77H

12   Alan Durning, Charts: Honest Elections Seattle Is An Incredible Bargain, *Sightline Institute*, May 4, 2015, https://perma.cc/TPW7-NN6Y

13   Alan Durning, Who Funds Seattle's Political Candidates?, *Sightline Institute*, Jul. 21, 2015, https://perma.cc/8K3B-EVEK

14   Ibid.

15   Margaret Morales, Seattles' Democracy Vouchers Are Changing the

Campaign Trail For Candidates And City Residents, *Sightline Institute*, Nov. 28, 2017, https://perma.cc/4Z75-ZDEZ

16   First Look: Seattle's Democracy Vouchers Program, *Win/Win Network*, *Every Voice Center*, Nov. 15, 2017, https://perma.cc/N745-T4ZD

17   Analysis performed by author on data from http://ethics.lacity.org. Analysis and methodology found here: tinyurl.com/ladvdata

18   Yes On H, *Austinites for Progressive Reform*, 2021, https://perma.cc/5597-72PJ

19   Monthly ranking of women in national parliaments, *IPU Parline*, https://perma.cc/R4T5-5TRM

20   Who Leads Us?, *Women Donors Network*, https://perma.cc/64E7-GAYD

21   Dr. Kira Sanbonmatsu, Why Women? The Impact of Women in Elective Office, *Political Parity*, https://perma.cc/V3M2-WKXA

22   Saskia Brechenmacher, Tackling Women's Underrepresentation in U.S. Politics: Comparative Perspectives from Europe, *Carnegie Endowment for International Peace*, https://perma.cc/RL8D-742N

23   Ibid.

24   Ibid.

25   Run for Something Community Impact Findings, *Avalanche*, Jan. 14, 2019, https://perma.cc/4KJN-K35A

26   Saskia Brechenmacher, Tackling Women's Underrepresentation in U.S. Politics: Comparative Perspectives from Europe, *Carnegie Endowment for International Peace*, https://perma.cc/RL8D-742N

27   Dr. Kira Sanbonmatsu, Money and Women Candidates, *Political Parity*, https://perma.cc/WQE4-78ZK

28   Saskia Brechenmacher, Tackling Women's Underrepresentation in U.S. Politics: Comparative Perspectives from Europe, *Carnegie Endowment for International Peace*, https://perma.cc/RL8D-742N

29   Ibid.

30   Martin Gilens and Benjamin I. Page, Testing Theories of American Politics: Elites, Interest Groups, and Average Citizens, *Cambridge University Press*, Sep. 18, 2014, https://perma.cc/4E3K-M8V2

31   *FollowTheMoney.org*, https://perma.cc/F5EG-6PES

MONEY IN POLITICS

32   2020 election to cost $14 billion, blowing away spending records, *Center for Responsive Politics*, Oct. 28, 2020, https://perma.cc/F4CY-L85F

33   Election Trends, *Center for Responsive Politics*, 2020, https://perma.cc/4T K5-3A5Y

34   Cost of Election, *Center for Responsive Politics*, 2020, https://perma.cc/7Z 94-KEUZ

35   2020 election to cost $14 billion, blowing away spending records, *Center for Responsive Politics*, Oct. 28, 2020, https://perma.cc/F4CY-L85F

36   15 states: Illinois, California, New York, Florida, Texas, Pennsylvania, New Jersey, Missouri, Virginia, Georgia, Tennessee, Michigan, Massachusetts, Wisconsin, Ohio

37   4 states: Vermont, Delaware, Alaska, and North Dakota

38   *FollowTheMoney.org*, https://perma.cc/ABD2-B5C7

39   *FollowTheMoney.org*, https://perma.cc/F5EG-6PES

40   Michael Barbaro, Bloomberg Spent $102 Million to Win 3rd Term, *The New York Times*, Nov. 27, 2009, https://perma.cc/8N4F-CQ4C

41   Lightfoot for Chicago D-2 Quarterly Report, *Illinois Stateboard of Elections*, https://perma.cc/7DN2-S734, https://perma.cc/XUF8-M63W, https://p erma.cc/2BZ6-G3PL, https://perma.cc/ZE2P-4G77

42   Contributions and Expenses Report, *Nevada Secretary of State*, https://per ma.cc/7Y3B-7YCR

43   *New York State Board of Elections*, https://perma.cc/T2Z3-HBL5

44   Real Gross Domestic Product, *Federal Reserve Economic Data*, 2020, https://perma.cc/FS5B-QY6W

45   Road Salt: Winter's $2.3 Billion Game Changer, *NBC News*, Feb. 19, 2015, https://perma.cc/2YDY-GWKW

46   Total Gross Domestic Product for Chicago-Naperville-Elgin, *Federal Reserve Economic Data*, 2020, https://perma.cc/A5NX-ZDEW

47   Chart sources: Governor Newsom Signs 2019-20 State Budget, *Office of Governor Gavin Newsom*, Jun. 27, 2019, https://perma.cc/WNB5-NLCZ; Denise Coffey, Frito Lay's Go-To Potato Guy, *Hartford Courant*, Jul. 31, 2018, https://perma.cc/C4HF-2QL7

48   Adam Bonica, Professional Networks, Early Fundraising, and Electoral Success, *Election Law Journal*, Dec. 29, 2016, https://perma.cc/BRJ3-A6BC

49   Isaac Arnsdorf, Trump won with half as much money as Clinton raised, *Politico*, Dec. 8, 2016, https://perma.cc/GV2N-6QRX

50   Maggie Koerth, How Money Affects Elections, *FiveThirtyEight*, Sep. 10, 2018, https://perma.cc/X8UU-MGHN

51   Adam Bonica, Professional Networks, Early Fundraising, and Electoral Success, *Election Law Journal*, Dec. 29, 2016, https://perma.cc/BRJ3-A6BC

52   Run for Something Community Impact Findings, *Avalanche*, Jan. 14, 2019, https://perma.cc/4KJN-K35A

53   Monetary Competitiveness in State Legislative Races, *FollowTheMoney.org*, https://perma.cc/4G2W-4FNL

54   Dr. Kira Sanbonmatsu, Money and Women Candidates, *Political Parity*, https://perma.cc/WQE4-78ZK

55   Seth Ferranti, Why Millenials Don't Run for Office, *Vice*, Jan. 30, 2017, https://perma.cc/Q3YN-VNWH

56   Adam Bonica, Professional Networks, Early Fundraising, and Electoral Success, *Election Law Journal*, Dec. 29, 2016, https://perma.cc/BRJ3-A6 BC; Membership of the 116th Congress, *Congressional Research Service*, Dec. 17, 2020, https://perma.cc/KXM6-RJCY

57   Public Esteem for Military Still High, *Pew Research Center*, Jul. 11, 2013, https://perma.cc/P4UU-328J

58   Adam Bonica, Professional Networks, Early Fundraising, and Electoral Success, *Election Law Journal*, Dec. 29, 2016, https://perma.cc/BRJ3-A6BC

59   Lukas Audackis, Richard Cracknell, Social background of MPs 1979-2019, *House of Commons Library*, Mar. 27, 2020, https://perma.cc/W795-LGRR

60   Adam Bonica, Professional Networks, Early Fundraising, and Electoral Success, *Election Law Journal*, Dec. 29, 2016, https://perma.cc/BRJ3-A6BC

61   Ibid.

62   Ibid.

63   Quoctrung Bui, Map: The Most Common Job In Every State, *NPR*, Feb. 5, 2015, https://perma.cc/KQG3-37BF

64   Contribution Limits, *Federal Elections Commission*, https://perma.cc/XJZ 9-R3XX

65   Ryan Grim and Sabrina Siddiqui, Call Time For Congress Shows How Fundraising Dominates Bleak Work Life, *HuffPost*, Jan. 8, 2013, https://p erma.cc/GFB4-FJX6

66   Congressional Fundraising: Last Week Tonight with John Oliver (HBO), *YouTube*, Apr. 3, 2016, https://perma.cc/F5XW-MZJY

67   Mark C. Alexander, Let Them Do Their Jobs, *Loyola University Chicago Law Journal*, Oct. 4, 2005, https://perma.cc/VR66-J3C5

68   Ibid.

69   Congressional Fundraising: Last Week Tonight with John Oliver (HBO), *YouTube*, Apr. 3, 2016, https://perma.cc/F5XW-MZJY

70   Ibid.

71   Ibid.

72   Ibid.

73   Mark C. Alexander, Let Them Do Their Jobs, *Loyola University Chicago Law Journal*, Oct. 4, 2005, https://perma.cc/VR66-J3C5

74   Ibid.

75   Ibid.

76   Ibid.

77   Incumbent Advantage, *Center for Responsive Politics*, 2018, https://perma.cc/9SH3-LHPP

78   Andrew Mayersohn, Donor demographics: old white guys edition, part III, *Center for Responsive Politics*, Jun. 30, 2015, https://perma.cc/9YQX-XPHH

79   Sean McElwee et al., Whose Voice, Whose Choice?, *Demos*, 2016, https://perma.cc/JZ9Y-ARY4

80   Ibid.

81   Naila Awan and Liz Kennedy, The Racial Equity Impact of Secret Political Spending by Government Contractors, *Demos*, Sep. 2, 2015, https://perma.cc/3V6Z-SGAL

82   Sabri Siraj, Money in Politics: a Barrier to Civil Rights Progress in the 21st Century, *People For The American Way*, Jun. 15, 2016, https://perma.cc/P6JM-SEDP

83   Andrew Mayersohn, Donor demographics: old white guys edition, part III, *Center for Responsive Politics*, Jun. 30, 2015, https://perma.cc/9YQX-XPHH

84   Incumbent Advantage, *Center for Responsive Politics*, 2018, https://perma.cc/9SH3-LHPP

85 Sean McElwee et al., Whose Voice, Whose Choice?, *Demos*, 2016, https://p
    erma.cc/JZ9Y-ARY4

86 Ibid.

87 Ibid.

88 Ibid.

89 Andrew Mayersohn, Donor demographics: old white guys edition, part
    III, *Center for Responsive Politics*, Jun. 30, 2015, https://perma.cc/9YQX-X
    PHH

90 2014-2018 Median Age in the United States by County, *United States
    Census Bureau*, Dec. 19, 2019, https://perma.cc/P2EZ-G86Q

91 National Exit Polls: How Different Groups Voted, *The New York Times*,
    https://perma.cc/4HV9-YAY7

92 The Generation Gap in American Politics, *Pew Research Center*, Mar. 1,
    2018, https://perma.cc/PBQ7-YBH9

93 Sean McElwee et al., Whose Voice, Whose Choice?, *Demos*, 2016, https://p
    erma.cc/JZ9Y-ARY4

94 Ibid.

95 Ibid.

96 Steve Israel: Confessions of a Congressman, *The New York Times*, Jan. 8,
    2016, https://perma.cc/HXX6-TM4P

97 Congressional Fundraising: Last Week Tonight with John Oliver (HBO),
    YouTube, Apr. 3, 2016, https://perma.cc/F5XW-MZJY

98 Barack Obama, *The Audacity of Hope*, 2006

99 Douglas D. Roscoe and Shannon Jenkins, A Meta-Analysis of Campaign
    Contributions' Impact on Roll Call Voting, *Social Science Quarterly*, Mar.
    2005, https://perma.cc/E96K-EG5U

100 Michael J. Barber, Representing the Preferences of Donors, Partisans,
    and Voters in the US Senate, *Public Opinion Quarterly*, Mar. 15, 2016,
    https://perma.cc/8DDT-29JK

101 Ibid.

102 Martin Gilens and Benjamin I. Page, Testing Theories of American Politics:
    Elites, Interest Groups, and Average Citizens, *Cambridge University Press*,
    Sep. 18, 2014, https://perma.cc/4E3K-M8V2

103 Sean McElwee et al., Whose Voice, Whose Choice?, *Demos*, 2016, https://p
    erma.cc/JZ9Y-ARY4

104 *American National Election Studies,* https://perma.cc/3ZAZ-P77H

105 Are Government Officials Crooked 1958-2014, *American National Election Studies;* https://perma.cc/RJ3Z-PVFY, Trust in Government Index 1958-2016, *American National Election Studies,* https://perma.cc/D7Z 5-YUYV; External Political Efficacy, *American National Election Studies,* https://perma.cc/U2K2-HRVC

106 Nicholas Confessore and Megan Thee-Brenan, Polls Shows Americans Favor an Overhaul of Campaign Financing, *The New York Times,* Jun. 2, 2015, https://perma.cc/3C6E-T3KZ

107 Lee Drutman, How Hatred Came To Dominate American Politics, *FiveThirtyEight,* Oct. 5, 2020, https://perma.cc/2Y8W-43KU

A BRIEF HISTORY OF CAMPAIGN FINANCE

108 The New York Life Contributed $48,000 To The Republican Campaign Funds In 1904, *The Daily Sun,* Sep. 16, 1905, https://perma.cc/XE5K-B4 YN

109 Robert E. Mutch, Buying the Vote, *Oxford University Press,* 2014

110 Ibid.

111 Ibid.

112 National Publicity Law To Be Pressed, *The New York Times,* Nov. 27, 1908, https://perma.cc/V9RZ-9NEC; Robert E. Mutch, Buying the Vote, *Oxford University Press,* 2014

113 Robert E. Mutch, Buying the Vote, *Oxford University Press,* 2014

114 Ibid.

115 The President's Apathy, *The New York Times,* Nov. 27, 1908, https://perma.cc/7UGN-ZEGK

116 Robert E. Mutch, Buying the Vote, *Oxford University Press,* 2014

117 The President's Apathy, *The New York Times,* Nov. 27, 1908, https://perma.cc/7UGN-ZEGK

118 Robert E. Mutch, Buying the Vote, *Oxford University Press,* 2014

119 Ibid.

120 Ibid.

121 Revision of Federal Corrupt Practices Act, *CQ Press,* https://perma.cc/S2 27-GPNW

122 Robert E. Mutch, Buying the Vote, *Oxford University Press,* 2014

123 Ibid.

124 1907 Theodore Roosevelt - Campaign Finance Reform, *State of the Union History*, Aug. 19, 2015, https://perma.cc/J6M4-MAT9

125 Ibid.

126 Theodore Roosevelt, Seventh Annual Message, *The American Presidency Project*, Dec. 3, 1907, https://perma.cc/SJD6-GB87

127 Robert E. Mutch, Buying the Vote, *Oxford University Press*, 2014

128 Theodore Roosevelt, Seventh Annual Message, *The American Presidency Project*, Dec. 3, 1907, https://perma.cc/SJD6-GB87

129 Robert E. Mutch, Buying the Vote, *Oxford University Press*, 2014

130 Ibid.

131 The Federal Election Campaign Laws: A Short History, *Federal Elections Commission*, https://perma.cc/P3YM-XSZX

132 Robert E. Mutch, Buying the Vote, *Oxford University Press*, 2014

133 Ibid.

134 Ibid.

135 Ibid.

136 Robert E. Mutch, Buying the Vote, *Oxford University Press*, 2014; Note: Technically the PCF was passed in 1966, then repealed, then reinstated in 1971

137 Presidential Election Campaign Fund Tax Check-Off Chart, *Federal Elections Commission*, Mar. 26, 2021, https://perma.cc/SKC4-ME6E

138 Robert E. Mutch, Buying the Vote, *Oxford University Press*, 2014

139 Obama opts out of public financing, *NBC News*, Jun. 19, 2008, https://perma.cc/SZ5H-7HJA

140 Kathy Kiely, Public campaign financing is so broken that candidates turned down $292 million in free money, *The Washington Post*, Feb. 9, 2016, https://perma.cc/7QFG-HFHR

141 Obama opts out of public financing, *NBC News*, Jun. 19, 2008, https://perma.cc/SZ5H-7HJA

142 Robert E. Mutch, Buying the Vote, *Oxford University Press*, 2014

143 Max Greenwood, Biden campaign, DNC raise record $364.5 million in August, *The Hill*, Sep. 2, 2020, https://perma.cc/TD9W-6NQ3; Anthony Raimondi, How Much Money Did Democrats, Joe Biden Raise In

September? A Look At The Numbers As Election Day Looms, *International Business Times*, Sep. 15, 2020, https://perma.cc/UM2J-PDBF

144 Robert E. Mutch, Buying the Vote, *Oxford University Press*, 2014

145 Ibid.

146 Ibid.

147 5 corporations: Gulf Oil, Goodyear Tire & Rubber, Phillips Petroleum, Minnesota Mining & Manufacturing, and Ashland Oil

148 Our Impact, *Common Cause*, https://perma.cc/LQ2P-5G75

149 Kate Pickert, Campaign Financing: A Brief History, *Time*, Jun. 30, 2008, https://perma.cc/Q8PY-JX5E

150 The First 10 Years, *The Federal Elections Commission*, Apr. 14, 1985, https://perma.cc/YG3B-QJL3

151 Ibid.

152 Robert E. Mutch, Buying the Vote, *Oxford University Press*, 2014

153 Ibid.

154 Robert E. Mutch, Buying the Vote, *Oxford University Press*, 2014

155 Michelle Ye Hee Lee, Senate confirms three FEC commissioners, restoring full slate for the first time since 2017, *The Washington Post*, Dec. 9, 2020, https://perma.cc/7CPQ-3Z2Q, Lisa J. Stevenson et al., Memorandum: Status of Enforcement—Fiscal Year 2020, Second Quarter, *Federal Elections Commission*, May. 5, 2020, https://perma.cc/BZQ2-M9SD

156 Robert E. Mutch, Buying the Vote, *Oxford University Press*, 2014

157 Ibid.

158 3 groups: Common Cause, the Center for Public Financing of Elections, and the League of Women Voters

159 Robert E. Mutch, Buying the Vote, *Oxford University Press*, 2014

160 Ibid.

161 Ibid.

162 Ibid.

163 Beth Rowen, Campaign-Finance Reform: History and Timeline, *Infoplease*, Feb. 28, 2017, https://perma.cc/C2JF-T2UX

164 Robert E. Mutch, Buying the Vote, *Oxford University Press*, 2014

165 Ibid.

166 Ibid.

167 Ibid.

168 Ibid.

169 Ibid.

170 Ibid.

171 Ibid.

172 Eric Marx, State Bans On Soft Money, *The Center for Public Integrity*, May. 19, 2014, https://perma.cc/AB6J-KWJN

173 Robert E. Mutch, Buying the Vote, *Oxford University Press*, 2014

174 Thomas B. Edsall, Reagan Campaign Gearing Up Its 'Soft Money' Machine for '84, *The Washington Post*, Nov. 27, 1983, https://perma.cc/P468-NEZP

175 Robert E. Mutch, Buying the Vote, *Oxford University Press*, 2014

176 Colorado Republican Federal Campaign Committee et al. v. Federal Elections Commission, *Legal Information Institute*, https://perma.cc/UKE5-T6T5

177 Robert E. Mutch, Buying the Vote, *Oxford University Press*, 2014

178 Ibid.

179 Ibid.

180 Kate Pickert, Campaign Financing: A Brief History, *Time*, Jun. 30, 2008, https://perma.cc/Q8PY-JX5E

181 Bush Signs Campaign Finance Reform Law, *Fox News*, Mar. 27, 2002, https://perma.cc/4AM9-ZSMQ

182 Robert E. Mutch, Buying the Vote, *Oxford University Press*, 2014

183 Kevin Drew, Campaign finance highlights next Supreme Court session, *CNN*, Jun. 29, 2003, https://perma.cc/B59L-4UBR

184 Robert E. Mutch, Buying the Vote, *Oxford University Press*, 2014; Mc-Connell v. Federal Elections Commission, *Justia*, https://perma.cc/L7KU-QWK5

185 Robert E. Mutch, Buying the Vote, *Oxford University Press*, 2014

186 Ibid.

187 Ibid.

188 Who are the Biggest Donors?, *Center for Responsive Politics*, 2020, https://perma.cc/TKY3-7ENG

189 Robert E. Mutch, Buying the Vote, *Oxford University Press*, 2014

190 FEC v. Wisconsin Right to Life, *Federal Elections Commission*, Aug. 1, 2007, https://perma.cc/H87J-H6Y5

191 Federal Election Commission v. Wisconsin Right to Life, *FindLaw*, https://perma.cc/ZDZ6-35K3

192 Citizens United v. FEC, *Federal Elections Commission*, Feb. 1, 2010, https://perma.cc/Z7AF-B72U

193 Ibid.

194 Ibid.

195 Austin v. Michigan State Chamber of Commerce, *Federal Elections Commission*, https://perma.cc/Z8LR-9KQS; McConnell v. Federal Elections Commission, *Justia*, https://perma.cc/L7KU-QWK5

196 Robert E. Mutch, Buying the Vote, *Oxford University Press*, 2014

197 SpeechNow.org v. FEC (Appeals court), *Federal Elections Commission*, May 3, 2010, https://perma.cc/E5HS-3PX7

198 Robert E. Mutch, Buying the Vote, *Oxford University Press*, 2014

199 Ibid.

200 Ibid.

201 Interview with Commissioner Ellen Weinraub via Zoom, November 10, 2020

202 Ibid.

203 Ibid.

204 Robert E. Mutch, Buying the Vote, *Oxford University Press*, 2014

205 2006 Outside Spending, by Group, *Center for Responsive Politics*, https://perma.cc/ED7R-87TA

206 2014 Outside Spending, by Group, *Center for Responsive Politics*, https://perma.cc/Z4J6-7AUC

207 Ian Vandewalker and Lawrence Norden, Getting Foreign Funds Out Of America's Elections, *Brennan Center for Justice*, 2018, https://perma.cc/AZ9R-5EHN

PUBLIC CAMPAIGN FINANCE PROGRAMS

208 History of the CFB, *New York City Campaign Finance Board*, https://perma.cc/K53G-A9XJ

209 Ibid.

210 How It Works, *New York City Campaign Finance Board*, https://perma.cc/83SR-DU3P

211 Impact of Public Funds, *New York City Campaign Finance Board*, https://perma.cc/BNN2-BBW7

212 J. David Goodman, Mayor de Blasio, Receiving Maximum City Funds, Agrees to Debate, *The New York Times*, Aug. 3, 2017, https://perma.cc/V3U9-4KHR

213 Keeping Democracy Strong: NYC's Campaign Finance Program in the 2017 Citywide Elections, *New York City Campaign Finance Board*, Aug. 30, 2018, https://perma.cc/W3NT-WV38

214 Ibid.

215 Benefits, *New York City Campaign Finance Board*, https://perma.cc/5CEY-78R2

216 Ibid.

217 Maine Clean Election Act, *Maine Commission on Governmental Ethics & Election Practices*, https://perma.cc/XV7L-R9B2

218 Maine Clean Election Act Overview 2002-2018, *Maine Commission on Governmental Ethics & Election Practices*, https://perma.cc/63LR-6ZYY

219 From The State House: Entire country should adopt Maine-style Clean Elections, *centralmaine.com*, Nov. 16, 2013, https://perma.cc/7VWM-2YY8

220 'More important than ever' to preserve, strengthen Clean Elections, *Bangor Daily New*, Oct. 2, 2013, https://perma.cc/3Q8P-BFGK

221 Alan Durning, Charts: Honest Elections Seattle Is An Incredible Bargain, *Sightline Institute*, May 4, 2015, https://perma.cc/TPW7-NN6Y; See the FAQ for an explanation of program cost. Image of a democracy voucher from Kevin Damp

222 Interview with Alan Durning via Zoom, September 24, 2020

223 A Tradition of Independence, *Washington Secretary of State*, https://perma.cc/5LRJ-6YG9

224 Seattle Democracy Voucher Program Evaluation, *BERK, City of Seattle Ethics and Elections Commission*, Apr. 20, 2018, https://perma.cc/6GCV-GZT3; 2019 Election Cycle Evaluation, *Seattle Ethics and Elections Commision*, Jul. 2020, https://perma.cc/X9NV-FEVZ

225 Brian J. McCabe and Jennifer A. Heerwig, Diversifying the Donor Pool: How Did Seattle's Democracy Voucher Program Reshape Participation in Municipal Campaign Finance?, *Election Law Journal*, Dec. 12, 2019, https://perma.cc/U6FW-8RZ5

226 Ibid.

227 Interview with Alan Durning via Zoom, September 24, 2020

228 Email from Andrew Grant Houston campaign

229 Seattle Democracy Voucher Program Evaluation, *BERK, City of Seattle Ethics and Elections Commission*, Apr. 20, 2018, https://perma.cc/6GCV-GZT3

230 Mark C. Alexander, Let Them Do Their Jobs, *Loyola University Chicago Law Journal*, Oct. 4, 2005, https://perma.cc/VR66-J3C5

231 Chris Jackson, Americans report a bipartisan desire for transparent political financing laws, *Ipsos*, Feb. 18, 2019, https://perma.cc/EHF3-2R87; Nikoel Hytrek, Poll: Campaign Finance Reform Resonates With All Voters, *Iowa Starting Line*, Sep. 11, 2019, https://perma.cc/58US-SBN4

232 Lauren Gambino, 'Not the billionaires': why small-dollar donors are Democrats' new powerhouse, *The Guardian*, Mar. 10, 2009, https://perma.cc/W7Q3-9BFF

233 Alan Durning, Democracy Vouchers Are Fraud-Repellent, *Sightline Institute*, Apr. 30, 2015, https://perma.cc/EX2U-XB8B

234 Democracy Voucher Program Data, *Seattle.gov*, 2021, https://perma.cc/G64J-JSZZ

235 Daniel Beekman, Seattle to drop charges in 'democracy voucher' alleged cheating case if former candidate adheres to deal, *The Seattle Times*, Apr. 6, 2018, https://perma.cc/J8KQ-LMFY

236 Bob Young, Seattle candidate accused of defrauding first-in-nation democracy-voucher program, *The Seattle Times*, Aug. 17, 2017, https://perma.cc/M4GV-ZFWC

237 Democracy Voucher Program: Biennial Report 2017, *Seattle Ethics & Elections Commission*, 2017, https://perma.cc/NJ3A-N3NF

238 Democracy Voucher Program: Biennial Report 2019, *Seattle Ethics & Elections Commission*, 2019, https://perma.cc/5K5T-P6EK

239 Analysis performed by author: https://perma.cc/KWP9-SCUV

240 Alan Durning, Charts: Honest Elections Seattle Is An Incredible Bargain, *Sightline Institute*, May 4, 2015, https://perma.cc/TPW7-NN6Y

241 https://perma.cc/L2FC-7WWK

242 Eric M. Johnson, Seattle City Council repeals 'head tax' weeks after enactment, *Reuters*, Jun. 12, 2018, https://perma.cc/ELE2-VU6J

243 Ibid.

244 Ibid.

245 Mike Baker, Amazon Tests 'Soul of Seattle' With Deluge of Election Cash, *The New York Times*, Oct. 30, 2019, https://perma.cc/3RUD-S5XS

246 City elections in Seattle, Washington (2019), *Ballotpedia*, https://perma.cc /5MR4-KP8L

247 Mike Baker, Amazon Tests 'Soul of Seattle' With Deluge of Election Cash, *The New York Times*, Oct. 30, 2019, https://perma.cc/3RUD-S5XS

248 Nick Nyhart and Adam Eichen, Grassroots Money Beats Amazon in Seattle, *The American Prospect*, Nov. 15, 2019, https://perma.cc/T6ML-5 PHT

249 Ibid.

250 Ballot return statistics: November 2019 General Election, *King County Elections*, Dec. 7, 2019, https://perma.cc/D5RZ-922H

251 Interview with Alan Durning via Zoom, September 24, 2020

252 Ibid.

253 Analogy from Andrew Allison of Austinites for Progressive Reform. https://perma.cc/BUE9-MPBR

254 Nick Nyhart and Adam Eichen, Grassroots Money Beats Amazon in Seattle, *The American Prospect*, Nov. 15, 2019, https://perma.cc/T6ML-5 PHT

255 Daniel Person, Jon Grant Says He's Signing Seattle's Homeless Up for Democracy Vouchers, *Seattle Weekly*, Mar. 14, 2017, https://perma.cc/A5 H7-FFHF

256 Jin Zhao, Why We Should Care About The Homeless Vote, *National Coalition for the Homeless*, Aug. 9, 2012, https://perma.cc/VK2D-PKJY

257 Analysis performed by author on data from http://ethics.lacity.org. Analysis and methodology found here: tinyurl.com/ladvdata

258 Brian J. McCabe and Jennifer A. Heerwig, Diversifying the Donor Pool: How Did Seattle's Democracy Voucher Program Reshape Participation in Municipal Campaign Finance?, *Election Law Journal*, Dec. 12, 2019, https://perma.cc/U6FW-8RZ5

259 James L. Buckely et al., Appellants v. Francis R. Valeo, Secretary of the United States Senate, et al., (two cases), *Legal Information Institute*, https://p erma.cc/G8T4-FJUS

260 Daggett v. Commission on Governmental Ethics & Election Practices, *Brennan Center for Justice*, Mar. 7, 2000, https://perma.cc/55YR-X5KX

261 *Citizens Clean Elections Commission*, https://perma.cc/ME2V-PTQN

262 Arizona Free Enterprise v. Bennett; McComish v. Bennett (consolidated), *Legal Information Institute*, https://perma.cc/D3QP-UUUF

263 Ibid.

264 Arizona Free Enterprise Club's Freedom Club Pac v. Bennett, *CaseText*, https://perma.cc/VAG7-F9LG

265 Ibid.

266 What We Do, *Citizens Clean Elections Commission*, https://perma.cc/GG4 Y-Q4GK

267 Elster v. City of Seattle, *Pacific Legal Foundation*, Jun. 28, 2017, https://pe rma.cc/CX3B-B4FR

268 Gene Johnson, Lawsuit challenges Seattle campaign 'democracy vouchers', *The Seattle Times*, Jun. 28 , 2017, https://perma.cc/ZU3S-R89R

269 Gene Johnson, Judge upholds Seattle's novel 'democracy' campaign-finance vouchers, *The Seattle Times*, Nov. 3, 2017, https://perma.cc/ TM7L-J4ZP

270 Daniel Beekman, Washington state Supreme Court unanimously upholds Seattle's pioneering 'democracy vouchers', *The Seattle Times*, Jul. 11, 2019, https://perma.cc/5A53-6VJQ

271 Elster and Pynchon v. City of Seattle, *Pacific Legal Foundation*, Jul. 11, 2019, https://perma.cc/4C9H-4MY3

272 Docket for 19-608, *Supreme Court of the United States*, Nov. 12, 2019, https://perma.cc/M7ZD-7ZKX

BUILDING A DEMOCRACY VOUCHERS PROGRAM

273 Interview with Alan Durning via Zoom, September 24, 2020

274 Who can and can't contribute, *Federal Elections Commission*, https://perm a.cc/LNM7-V6VU

275 Democracy Voucher Program Application, *Seattle Ethics & Elections Commission*, https://perma.cc/3KA3-UCCJ

276 Amy Radil, Lost your democracy vouchers, Seattle? Campaigns will help you out, *NPR*, Mar. 12, 2021, https://perma.cc/TAT2-35EX

277 Thomas Latkowski and Michael Brennan, Public Payments Platform, *Democracy Policy Network*, https://perma.cc/G8LB-L38A

278 About the Program, *Seattle.gov*, https://perma.cc/MRS7-6W8Q; See the FAQ for an explanation of program cost

279 Washington State-Provided Campaign Financing Funded by a Non-Resident Sales Tax, Initiative 1464 (2016), *Ballotpedia*, https://perma.cc/74Q7-VHUS

280 Daggett v. Commission on Governmental Ethics & Election Practices, *Brennan Center for Justice*, Mar. 7, 2000, https://perma.cc/55YR-X5KX

281 Alan Durning, Seattle Candidates, Meet Democracy Vouchers, *Sightline Institute*, Apr. 20, 2015, https://perma.cc/GJ4V-C4U3

282 In Seattle, voucher donation lists are available here: https://perma.cc/G64J-JSZZ

283 Democracy Voucher Program: Biennial Report 2017, *Seattle Ethics & Elections Commission*, 2017, https://perma.cc/NJ3A-N3NF

284 Ibid.

285 How do I use my Democracy Vouchers? (English Version), *Youtube*, https://perma.cc/Q9J5-2UHV

286 Internal Program Reports, *Seattle.gov*, https://perma.cc/9558-SPML

287 15 languages: Amharic, Cambodian, Chinese (Traditional and Simplified), English, Filipino, Korean, Lao, Oromo, Russian, Somali, Spanish, Thai, Tigrigna, Ukrainian, and Vietnamese

288 Democracy Voucher Program: Biennial Report 2019, *Seattle Ethics & Elections Commission*, 2019, https://perma.cc/5K5T-P6EK

289 California Proposition 68, Campaign Spending Limits (June 1988), *Ballotpedia*, https://perma.cc/3KRT-XHJ5

290 California Proposition 73, Limits on Campaign Donations (June 1988), *Ballotpedia*, https://perma.cc/2LAU-TVFF

291 *Buckley v. Valeo*, *Oyez*, https://perma.cc/2V76-22F6

292 Ibid.

293 More About Coordination, *Coordination Watch*, https://perma.cc/C9NC-TKA2

294 Components of an Effective Coordination Law, *Brennan Center for Justice*, May 2018, https://perma.cc/767N-BUN4

295 Ibid.

296 Components of an Effective Disclosure Law, *Brennan Center for Justice*, May 2018, https://perma.cc/D4AU-F2M5

297 Political Campaign Financing—Disclosures, *Washington State Legislature*, https://perma.cc/GZ2G-YNFN

298 Components of an Effective Disclosure Law, *Brennan Center for Justice*, May 2018, https://perma.cc/D4AU-F2M5

299 Brendan W. Donckers, and Hardeep Singh Rekhi, *Seattle Ethics & Elections Commission*, Aug. 5, 2019, https://perma.cc/HHP3-KPRU

300 Clean Campaigns Act, *Seattle City Council*, https://perma.cc/P82V-PAJ5

301 Ellen W. Weintraub, Taking On Citizens United, *New York Times*, Mar. 30, 2016, https://perma.cc/D44U-4AAV

302 Abdi Soltani, After Citizens United: A Different Path Forward, *Stanford Social Innovation Review*, Oct. 29, 2015, https://perma.cc/37MZ-YXZF

303 IRS Clarifies Tax on Executive Pay at Nonprofit Organizations, *Society for Human Resource Management*, Feb. 17, 2021, https://perma.cc/R84U-GVZD

CAMPAIGNING FOR DEMOCRACY VOUCHERS

304 South Dakota Revision of State Campaign Finance and Lobbying Laws, Initiated Measure 22 (2016), *Ballotpedia*, https://perma.cc/E2A7-2675

305 South Dakota GOP uses 'emergency' rules to repeal anti-corruption law, *CNN*, Feb. 2, 2017, https://perma.cc/TX6V-X969

306 David W. Moore, Widespread Public Support for Campaign Finance Reform, *Gallup*, Mar. 20, 2001, https://perma.cc/2U52-6VFM; Denver Nicks, Poll: Support for Campaign Finance Reform Strong in Key Senate Races, *Time*, Jul. 31, 2014, https://perma.cc/BC75-4D2G; Most Americans want to limit campaign spending, say big donors have greater political influence, *Pew Research Center*, May 8, 2018, https://perma.cc/P 9Q6-VTGU; Nikoel Hytrek, Poll: Campaign Finance Reform Resonates With All Voters, *Iowa Starting Line*, Sep. 11, 2019, https://perma.cc/58US-SBN4

307 Analysis performed by author on data from http://ethics.lacity.org. Analysis and methodology found here: tinyurl.com/ladvdata. These numbers

count matching funds as LA based non-special interest donations.

308 Adam Bonica, Professional Networks, Early Fundraising, and Electoral Success, *Election Law Journal*, Dec. 29, 2016, https://perma.cc/BRJ3-A6BC

309 Run for Something Community Impact Findings, *Avalanche*, Jan. 14, 2019, https://perma.cc/4KJN-K35A

310 Majority of Americans Support Campaign Finance Reform, *Ipsos*, Aug. 24, 2017, https://perma.cc/FMP7-RUSX

311 "Honest Elections Seattle" Initiative (I-122), *Seattle.gov*, https://perma.cc/3GTR-4FMP

TOWARD A DEEPER DEMOCRACY

312 Winston Churchill, Nov. 11, 1947, https://perma.cc/3R9J-L8FA

313 W.E.B. Du Bois, Black Reconstruction, *Harcourt, Brace and Company*, 1935, https://perma.cc/EZ7J-4T54

314 Gayatri Chakravorty Spivak et al., *Abolition Democracy*, Oct. 15, 2020, https://perma.cc/MM2B-S9K4

315 Allegra M. McLeod, Envisioning Abolition Democracy, *Harvard Law Review*, Apr. 10, 2019, https://perma.cc/73ZL-7ZN9

316 W.E.B. Du Bois, The Souls of Black Folks, *Oxford World's Classics*, 1903, https://perma.cc/9VMX-A52D

FREQUENTLY ASKED QUESTIONS

317 Nick Nyhart and Adam Eichen, Grassroots Money Beats Amazon in Seattle, *The American Prospect*, Nov. 15, 2019, https://perma.cc/T6ML-5PHT

318 Alan Durning, Charts: Honest Elections Seattle Is An Incredible Bargain, *Sightline Institute*, May 4, 2015, https://perma.cc/TPW7-NN6Y

319 Analysis performed by author: https://perma.cc/KWP9-SCUV

320 Democracy Voucher Program: Biennial Report 2019, *Seattle Ethics & Elections Commission*, 2019, https://perma.cc/5K5T-P6EK

321 Alan Durning, Charts: Honest Elections Seattle Is An Incredible Bargain, *Sightline Institute*, May 4, 2015, https://perma.cc/TPW7-NN6Y

322 Alan Durning, Democracy Vouchers Are Fraud-Repellent, *Sightline Institute*, Apr. 30, 2015, https://perma.cc/EX2U-XB8B

323 Democracy Voucher Program: Biennial Report 2017, *Seattle Ethics & Elections Commission*, 2017, https://perma.cc/NJ3A-N3NF

324 Seattle Democracy Voucher Program Evaluation, *BERK, City of Seattle Ethics and Elections Commission*, Apr. 20, 2018, https://perma.cc/6GCV-GZT3

325 South Dakota Revision of State Campaign Finance and Lobbying Laws, Initiated Measure 22 (2016), *Ballotpedia*, https://perma.cc/E2A7-2675; South Dakota GOP uses 'emergency' rules to repeal anti-corruption law, *CNN*, Feb. 2, 2017, https://perma.cc/TX6V-X969

326 Nicholas Confessore and Megan Thee-Brenan, Polls Shows Americans Favor an Overhaul of Campaign Financing, *The New York Times*, Jun. 2, 2015, https://perma.cc/3C6E-T3KZ

327 5 times: Seattle, Washington 2015 (passed, https://perma.cc/S2H2-QAX8), South Dakota 2016 (passed, https://perma.cc/E2A7-2675), Washington 2016 (failed, https://perma.cc/74Q7-VHUS), Albuquerque, New Mexico 2019 (failed, https://perma.cc/24J6-CS7Q), Austin, Texas 2021 (failed, https://perma.cc/ZA3K-SQJ2)

328 Mike Clark-Madison, May 1 Special Election Results: First Five Win, Last Three Lose, *Austin Chronicle*, May. 1, 2021, https://perma.cc/4REM-BG NJ

329 Nicholas Confessore and Megan Thee-Brenan, Polls Shows Americans Favor an Overhaul of Campaign Financing, *The New York Times*, Jun. 2, 2015, https://perma.cc/3C6E-T3KZ

About the Democracy Policy Network

This book is a project of the Democracy Policy Network's Open Government workshop. The Democracy Policy Network (DPN) is an interstate network that organizes policy support for the next generation of state leaders working to deepen democracy in statehouses across America. By organizing people to gather, package, organize, and amplify a transformative, deep-dive policy agenda spanning every state issue, we provide bold state leaders with the policy support they need to deepen democracy. DPN's Open Government workshop works to raise up policies related to opening up our government—our legislatures, elections, courts, and agencies—to more people in more ways. To learn more, visit www.DemocracyPolicy.network.

Made in the USA
Monee, IL
14 August 2021